DIVORCE:
A CLIENT'S GUIDE

- ILLINOIS EDITION -

by Sheila Simon

JUSTICE PUBLICATIONS®, INC.
529 Hampshire Street, Suite 609
Quincy, Illinois 62301

Copyright © 1993 by Justice Publications®, Inc.

Printed in the United States of America

ISBN 1-884177-01-8

2-1-893

TABLE OF CONTENTS

CHAPTER 1

INTRODUCTION

This book is designed to assist people who are in the process of getting a divorce, or who are thinking about getting a divorce. This book is not a do-it-yourself manual on how to get a divorce. Divorce law is very complicated, and the only way to make sure that your rights are protected in a divorce case is to have an attorney.

Illinois has a new law creating a "simplified" divorce process for some couples with no children and limited assets. But even if this simplified procedure can be used in your case, your best protection is to seek the advice of an attorney.[1]

Chapter 4 of this book contains some tips on how to find an attorney if you do not already have one. The remainder of this book helps you understand the legal process and what your lawyer is telling you, and helps you work effectively with your lawyer.

This book contains information on processes and questions that come up in most divorce cases. Because each couple is different, each divorce is different. There may be chapters in this book that deal with issues that are not present in your divorce, such as child custody, if you have no children.

You can pick out the chapters and sections that are meaningful to you without having to read the whole book. Your divorce may also involve issues that are not covered in this book. You will need to review those areas with your lawyer carefully, to make sure you understand those issues.

While friends and family can be helpful and supportive while you are getting your divorce, they can also be misleading. Myths about divorce law are very common. For example, many people believe that if title to a car is held in the wife's name then she will automatically receive the car as a part of the divorce. In Illinois, that is not necessarily the case.

Another frequently held myth is that a parent who is not current on a child support obligation loses visitation rights. Although the obligation and rights seem to go together logically, they are not linked in Illinois law.

You may also hear stories about people who were "taken to the cleaners" by their former spouses, or people who received very favorable divorce judgments. The best authority for this information is still your lawyer. Your lawyer is familiar with the laws of Illinois and with the judgments that are issued by the judges in your local courts.

Your lawyer has an obligation to represent you well. The stories of friends or family members about their divorces may be stretching the truth a bit, or leaving out an important detail that they do not wish to share with you.

The book contains several pages throughout for you to use in jotting down questions for your attorney or reminders for yourself. If you are borrowing this book from your attorney or your local library, you may wish to get out a few sheets of paper so you can note your questions before you forget them.

Some divorces are painful, some are pleasant. All of them are an important step in a person's life, a step that should be taken with great care, and with a thorough understanding of the processes and the possible outcomes.

1.   750 ILCS 5/451 et seq.

CHAPTER 2

A QUICK OVERVIEW OF THE DIVORCE PROCESS

Because each divorce involves different people and different disagreements, each divorce case takes its own unique path. Your lawyer is the only person who can predict how long your divorce will take and what issues will cause problems in the process—and even those predictions are just best guesses.

There are some general categories, however, into which your divorce may fall. Divorces can be obtained by default, meaning that the other party has failed to participate; they can be uncontested, meaning that the parties have reached agreement on the issues involved; and they can be contested, with disagreements over some or all issues involved.

A default divorce begins in the same way that any other divorce does: a petition for dissolution of marriage is filed at the courthouse. This petition is then served, with a summons, on the other spouse. The spouse has 30 days after he or she has been served to take some action in court, whether it be entering his or her appearance or responding to the allegations in the petition.

If the spouse fails to take any actin within the 30-day period, he or she can be held in default. Because the person has failed to answer within the time given, the judge can proceed to complete the case without the participation of that spouse. In such cases, both the ground for divorce and all the other issues involved in the divorce are presented to the judge at one hearing. The judge can then make a final judgment even without the presence of the other party.

An uncontested divorce is possible when the husband and wife agree on all the issues involved in the divorce. The first step in court in this type of divorce is also filing a petition. In uncontested cases, one spouse will often waive, in writing, the requirement of being served with a summons. The parties usually make their agreement final by preparing a marital settlement agreement and an agreement about custody issues, if necessary. Only one court hearing is scheduled in such cases. The judge is presented with the agreement of the parties and reviews it to make sure that it is fair, particularly if there are children involved.

Although most divorce cases end up with an agreement, they often begin with at least some disagreement. These cases are referred to as contested cases and begin with a petition for dissolution of marriage and with service of a summons and petition on the other spouse. The other spouse responds to the petition and may file his or her own counterpetition for dissolution of marriage.e If a counterpetition is filed, the first spouse will need to respond to that counterpetition.

In contested cases, there are often issues that must be resolved very quickly, such as who will stay in the house, who will care for the children, and whether either party will make payments to the other party until the divorce is final. It may be necessary to have a hearing on how these issues will be handled until the divorce is final. These contested cases also involve some discovery, which is a process used to find out information in order to prepare for further negotiations at a hearing.

In a contested divorce, there will usually be at least two hearings. The first hearing, often called the first-stage hearing, covers grounds for divorce. The second-stage hearing considers all others issues after grounds for divorce have been found.

The chart below summarizes the steps involved in the three general categories of divorce. As you can see, a default or uncontested divorce can move much more quickly than a contested divorce. The longer your divorce case lasts, the greater your frustrations and the higher your attorney's fees. These are important considerations in reviewing a reasonable offer of settlement in a divorce case.

DEFAULT	UNCONTESTED	CONTESTED
Petition	Petition	Petition
Service	Waive of Service	Service
Failure to	Marital Settlement	Response and
Respond	Agreement	Counterpetition
Hearing	Hearing	Response to Counterpetition
		Temporary Relief
		Discover
		First-stage Hearing
		Second-stage Hearing

CHAPTER 3

WHERE DO WE GET DIVORCE LAW?

Laws regarding marriage and divorce come from many different sources. Divorce law in the United States, like most of our other law, comes from England originally. But, as American culture is different from the British, American divorce law is also different from current English divorce law. Part of that difference is a result of changes that have taken place within our society, particularly the increase in the number of women in the paid workforce.

Because society's attitudes toward family structure have changed, and the laws have changed with those attitudes, the laws that apply to your divorce may not be the same laws that applied to a friend who was divorced 10 years ago, or a parent who was divorced 20 years ago.

The actual laws that apply to divorces come from four different sources: (a) statutes, (b) case law, (c) constitutions, and (d) local rules. Both the federal government and the state government have these sources of laws, but in general, the state laws are more important for family relationships.

Historically, the federal government has let the states decide for themselves the appropriate laws with regard to families. This is why each state varies from the others as to the laws that apply to a family situation.

Statutes are the source of law that we most often think of when considering the question of what is the law in a specific area. Both the federal and state government have statutes, which are passed by the legislature and signed by either the governor or president to become law. For example, the federal government has a statute preventing parental kidnapping,[1] and the state governments have a set of statutes regarding divorce and custody. State statutes set the grounds for getting a divorce and the guidelines for determining which parent will get custody of the child.

While the statutes that make the law are clear in many circumstances, there are often times when it is not clear how a statute should be applied in a certain set of circumstances.

Case law fills in those blanks. Case law refers to published cases that have been decided by appellate courts. These cases almost always involve a situation where it was not clear from the statutes how the dispute should have been resolved. The appeals court resolves the question for that particular issue, and if those circumstances should arise again, a trial judge familiar with that case will know how to decide the issue.

Of course, there are still gaps in the law. This is when you most need the assistance of an attorney. The lawyer's job is to be aware of the statutes and the cases that interpret those statutes, so that he or she can best advise you on how the law applies to your situation.

Constitutions also play a role in laws regarding family relationships. The Illinois and federal constitutions set out the broad principles on which our governments are based. For example, the amendments to the U.S. Constitution are the source of limitations upon the government's abilities to intrude into your family relationships.

Laws also set up procedural rules for how a case can be started and completed. The Illinois statutes will guide your lawyer in the process of obtaining jurisdiction (discussed in Chapter 7). Local rules, which are established by the courts in your area, may also govern the procedure of a case, such as when a motion or response must be filed, and when a judge will hear arguments on certain issues.

You will not need to know all the statutes and case law that apply to your particular situation. That is the job of your lawyer. Understanding these different sources of law, however, will help you to understand why there is not always an easy answer to the question, "What does the law say?"

1.   Parental Kidnapping Prevention Act of 1980, 38 USCA, Section 1738(a).

CHAPTER 4

HOW TO FIND AN ATTORNEY
IF YOU DON'T ALREADY HAVE ONE

Finding an attorney can be a difficult task. If you have already found your attorney, congratulations! You will not need to read this chapter. If you are still looking for an attorney, there are several methods you can use to find an attorney who is right for you.

One of the easiest ways is by looking in the yellow pages of your phone book. The lawyers will be listed under the heading of "Attorneys." Until recently, lawyers were not allowed to advertise for their services. Now that lawyers can advertise to some extent, some lawyers choose to advertise their services in the phone book. The ads in the phone book may include lists of areas of law in which the lawyer concentrates.

If you need an attorney to represent you in a divorce, you may want to check for attorneys who advertise that they work on divorce, family law, domestic relations, or custody. Many lawyers do not list areas of concentration in the phone book, so you may want to call those offices to find out whether or not they would handle such a case.

Another source for finding a lawyer is the Illinois Lawyer Referral Service. This service is run by the Illinois State Bar Association. The Lawyer Referral Service operates a toll-free line at (800) 252-8916. You can call the service, tell them the area in which you live and the type of legal problem you have. They will refer you to an attorney in your area who is willing to handle your kind of case.

The call to the Lawyer Referral Service is free. The cost for an initial consultation with the lawyer to whom you have been referred is $15.00 for the first half-hour consultation. Any arrangements for further consultation or representation would have to be made with the lawyer.

The advantage of the Lawyer Referral Service is that you most likely will be referred to someone who handles divorce cases, and the fee for the initial consultation is relatively low.

Probably the best way to find an attorney is by word-of-mouth. Cases involving family relationships may require that you discuss with your attorney details of your life that have previously been private. Because of that, you should try to find an attorney you trust and can be comfortable with.

If you have friends who have been through similar legal problems, ask them about their attorneys. You may be able to find a good attorney this way. The word-of-mouth method may help you avoid hiring an attorney who will not be right for you. You may also meet with more than one attorney to make some comparisons on your own. Paying for an initial meeting with a few attorneys may be a good investment if it helps you find the attorney who is right for you.

In some cases, there is one other option available to people of limited income. The federal government funds the Legal Services Corporation, which has offices nationwide. Many of these offices provide services to people involved in divorce cases. To find out whether your income and assets make you eligible for legal assistance services, call your local Legal Services office. The services provided vary from office to office. Where one office may handle any divorce, another office may work on cases only where minor children are involved.

Within Cook County, there are also additional organizations that provide legal services to people with limited income. An appendix at the end of this book has a list of agencies and phone numbers. If the agency you contact cannot assist you, ask whether there are any other agencies they know of that would be able to help.

CHAPTER 5

HOW TO WORK WITH YOUR ATTORNEY

Your attorney will ask you many questions about the facts involved in your particular case, and about what results you hope to achieve. It is also important for you to understand how your attorney works, so that you can work most effectively with him or her. Understanding some of the rules that govern a lawyer's conduct may help you to better understand your attorney.

One of the most important aspects of the attorney-client relationship is that of confidentiality. Your lawyer is required to keep information confidential unless you allow your lawyer to disclose that information.[1] How the attorney obtains information from you will have an impact on whether or not the information is confidential.

If you and your attorney are in the attorney's office with no other people present, information exchanged in that meeting will be confidential. If you and your attorney meet where other friends of yours are present, and you provide your attorney with information at that time, that information will not be confidential. That does not mean that your attorney will spread the information far and wide. It only means that the privilege your lawyer has to keep information confidential for you will not apply to those types of conversations.

Confidentiality is important because it means you can be free to discuss all aspects of your case with your lawyer, and your lawyer will not be forced to disclose any of those details later to anyone else.

The rules that govern lawyers also require a lawyer to explain to you all of the options involved in your case. Sometimes your lawyer may explain things to you that are very remote possibilities in your case. Your lawyer is doing this to make sure that you understand all of the options and are fully informed before you make decisions.

Rules that govern lawyers' conduct also require that they forward to you any offers for settlement of the case. This may mean, at some point during your case, that your lawyer will send you a letter or call you with an offer of settlement in the case that seems to be unacceptable to you. The lawyer is required to give you that information so that you can make the decision as to what is acceptable and what is unacceptable.

Your lawyer will usually tell you whether or not he recommends accepting any given settlement proposal. In that way, you and your lawyer can work together as a team to reach the best result possible in your case.

There are also rules that apply to how lawyers can communicate with other parties in the case.[2] For instance, if your spouse is represented by another lawyer, your lawyer will not be able to contact your spouse directly. Your lawyer will only be able to contact your spouse's attorney. Sometimes this requirement can make exchanging information a difficult process. The benefit of this rule, however, is that you are assured that your spouse's attorney will not contact you and try to persuade you to accept any deal that he or she may propose.

You will also want to make sure that you understand how your lawyer will be charging for his or her services, and what arrangements will need to be made for payment of other expenses in the case. You will want to know when your lawyer will charge you for his or her activities. For example, it is fairly standard for a lawyer to charge for his or her time spent traveling to and from the courthouse for a hearing, time spent in legal research on your case, time spent on the phone with you, and time spent on the phone with the opposing lawyer.

Your lawyer may also charge a higher rate for hearings than for work done in the office. Most attorneys will have a written agreement that explains what fees will be charged for what services. The agreement may also cover other aspects of how you and your attorney will work together.

Make sure that you read the document carefully. Ask questions if you do not understand the terms, so that you are fully informed before you commit yourself to the agreement.

Cases involving divorce and custody frequently involve other charges besides the ones you will pay to your attorney. There is usually a filing fee, as well as a fee for serving a summons on another party. Other costs depend upon your case and may include payment for transcribing a deposition, payment for a psychological evaluation of parents in a custody case, and payment for the valuation of property, business, or pension interests. In most cases, it is hard to predict in the beginning what these costs might be. You may wish to discuss these potential costs with your lawyer, so that you have an estimate of what you may have to pay later.

There are many other rules which govern an attorney in the practice of law that may have an impact on how you and your attorney work together. The main thing to remember, however, is that your attorney works for you. If you have any questions, ask your attorney. It is better to pay your attorney for a few minutes to explain the answer to a question than to run the risk of having your attorney miss important information in your case, and for you to spend needless hours worrying about it.

There are also some realistic limits on what your attorney can do for you. While your divorce is important to your attorney, it is probably not the only divorce he or she is working on at the time. There may be times when your attorney is working on another case and is not available to help you right away. Be sure to leave a message so your attorney can get back in touch as soon as possible.

1.   Illinois Rules of Professional Conduct, Rule 1.6.

2.   Illinois Rules of Professional Conduct, Rules 4.2 and 4.3.

NOTES

CHAPTER 6

DO YOU HAVE TO GET A DIVORCE?

In some instances when people are considering divorce, it is only one of the remedies available, and in some instances, because there has been no marriage, no divorce is necessary.

Without a valid marriage, there is no need for a divorce. This may sound basic, but different states have different laws on how people can become married. In particular, some states have what is referred to as a "common-law marriage". This means that if a couple lives together, and holds themselves out as a married couple for a certain length of time, they can be considered married. Illinois does not make any provisions in its laws for common-law marriages. It is possible, however, that a common-law marriage created in another state could be a valid marriage here in Illinois if the husband and wife were to move to Illinois.

One other unusual situation when a divorce is not the appropriate remedy, is that of annulment, also known as declaration of invalidity of marriage. Annulment is a legal procedure to have a marriage set aside.[1] Annulment is available only in limited circumstances involving fraud, duress, influence of alcohol or drugs, inability to consummate the marriage, lack of legal ability to marry, or marriage prohibited by law.

Another option not frequently used is that of legal separation. Legal separation is a way in which you can obtain many of the results that can be obtained through a divorce proceeding, without actually ending the marriage.[2] A legal separation can provide, for example, support payments from one party to the other. If obtaining health insurance is a problem, legal separation may allow one spouse to remain covered by the other spouse's group plan longer than in the case of a divorce, although not all insurance companies allow this. The reason most people do not choose legal separation is that it does not end the marriage, and the parties are not free to marry again.

One thing to keep in mind, even if you do not want a divorce, is that your spouse will probably be able to obtain one sooner or later. Pursuing a legal separation may not be wise if your spouse is determined to pursue a divorce.

It is also possible to use a divorce to try to reconcile the problems of the marriage. After a case for divorce has been filed, your lawyer can ask the judge to order a conciliation conference, where the parties would be required to attempt to work out their differences.[3] Of course a court-ordered conciliation conference is probably not the best way to patch up a marriage. Your attorney may be able to refer you to a local mental health counselor for other suggestions on marriage counseling, if that is what you need and want.

1.   750 ILCS 5/301.

2.   750 ILCS 5/402.

3.   750 ILCS 5/404.

CHAPTER 7
JURISDICTION

Jurisdiction roughly means the power of the court to act. In order for a court to order that a marriage has come to an end, the court must have jurisdiction over the marriage. For a court to order your spouse to do or not do something, the court must have jurisdiction over your spouse. The court must also have jurisdiction to decide issues of child custody, and to decide issues of financial obligations and property division.

In most cases, jurisdiction is fairly easy to obtain, and it is clear that the court either has or does not have jurisdiction to act. There are some problems, though, that can come up in the area of jurisdiction.

To obtain jurisdiction over your spouse, your lawyer will complete a form called a summons, and have the circuit clerk issue the summons. The summons, attached to a copy of the petition in your case, will be served by the sheriff or sheriff's deputy upon your spouse. In some counties, the sheriff's office will send a notice to your spouse asking him or her to come in to pick up the documents. Other counties make it a practice to personally deliver summons without any advance notice. Once your spouse has been served, the court, with a few exceptions, has jurisdiction to take action with regard to your spouse. If your divorce is a friendly one, and you will be proposing an agreement for the judge's approval, your spouse may wish to waive receiving a summons. This means that your spouse will sign a form stating that he or she agrees with the items that you have requested in your divorce, and has no objection to having the divorce proceed without a summons being served upon him or her.

If your spouse signs a waiver, he or she will not receive a summons from the sheriff. Use of a waiver can speed up the divorce process by a few weeks, and can eliminate the sheriff's charge for service of process.

The court will also need to have jurisdiction over your marriage in order to issue a divorce order. Where both parties have resided in Illinois for more than 90 days, which is the case in most Illinois divorces, there is no question that the court will have jurisdiction over the marriage.[1] If only one spouse lives in Illinois, the court will still have jurisdiction over the marriage.

If both of you were in Illinois for more than 90 days before the date that you filed for divorce, the court will have jurisdiction. If you have moved to Illinois and have lived in Illinois for 90 days by the time the court makes a decision in your case, the court has jurisdiction over the marriage.

Rules for jurisdiction over child custody issues and visitation issues are governed by the Uniform Child Custody Jurisdiction Act, usually referred to as the UCCJA.[2] Each state, including Illinois, has adopted this uniform law or something very close to it. The most basic test of the UCCJA is the home state of the child. If the child has lived in Illinois for six months before the action has been filed, Illinois will have jurisdiction. If the child has not lived in Illinois for the past six months, the UCCJA uses various considerations to make sure that the custody dispute is resolved in the state that has the most connections to the child.

There are also special rules for a court's power to make decisions on child support. Illinois statutes allow for several circumstances under which an Illinois court can order a noncustodial parent to pay support even though the court does not have jurisdiction over that person through the service of a summons in Illinois.[3]

When the court does not have the power to order a noncustodial parent in a different state to pay child support, you may be able to work through an interstate system for enforcement of child support. See Chapter 15 for more information on child support issues.

There are also some situations where a court does not have jurisdiction over a person because no summons has ever been served, but the court can obtain jurisdiction over the person's property that has been left in the state of Illinois, whether that property is real estate or other tangible items. This method can be useful in getting the attention of a spouse who is trying to avoid being part of a legal action.

After reading this chapter, you should have some idea of the different kinds of jurisdiction that a court can have, and the different areas where problems may arise. If the jurisdiction questions in your case are more complicated than the explanations provided here, be sure to ask your attorney to explain them to you.

1.   750 ILCS 5/401.

2.   750 ILCS 35.

3.   750 ILCS 5/2-209.

NOTES

CHAPTER 8

GROUNDS FOR DIVORCE

Generations ago a divorce was difficult to obtain. The law made it difficult by imposing requirements on the reasons one could get a divorce. These requirements for divorce are referred to as grounds for divorce. The laws in most states have gradually grown to be less demanding, and allow people to get divorced without extensive proof on particular grounds.

Some states have eliminated the requirement that there be grounds in order to grant a divorce. Illinois is in between. Illinois has 11 grounds for divorce that are similar to the older requirements for divorce, and Illinois has one "no-fault" divorce provision that applies in certain circumstances.[1] These grounds are listed in 750 ILCS 5/401, which is quoted in Appendix No. 1 of this book.

One of these grounds or reasons for divorce must be proven to the judge before a divorce can be granted. Probably the two most common grounds for divorce in Illinois now are mental cruelty and irreconcilable differences (the no-fault option).

To get a divorce based on mental cruelty, you must be able to prove to the judge that your spouse, without cause or provocation by you, has been guilty of extreme mental cruelty toward you on more than one occasion and that you suffered some physical or mental effects. Although this sounds severe, there is a growing trend toward a lenient interpretation of those terms. Often it will be enough to prove that you and your spouse had many disagreements; that you did not provoke the disagreements; that you suffered from stress, sleeplessness, weight loss, or other problems as a result; and that you have felt better since your separation.

Since each judge may require a slightly different level of proof, your lawyer will tell you what to expect from the judge who will be hearing your case. Your lawyer will probably review with you, in advance of the hearing, the testimony that will be required from you in order to obtain a divorce based on mental cruelty. There are also some judges who will, if both spouses are present, allow one spouse to concede that he or she has been mentally cruel, and avoid having the other spouse testify as to any details.

The other frequently used ground for divorce in Illinois is that of irreconcilable differences. It is sometimes referred to as a no-fault divorce.[2] To prove these grounds for divorce, you must be able to prove that (1) you and your spouse have lived separate and apart for two years, (2) that irreconcilable differences have caused an irretrievable breakdown of your marriage, and (3) that future attempts to repair the marriage would not be practical, and would not be in the family's best interest. The requirements boil down to proving that the marriage has broken beyond repair, where the spouses have lived separately.

The two-year time limit for living separate and apart can be reduced to six months if both parties agree, either in writing or in testimony before the court, that they wish to waive the two-year requirement. Any time that spouses stay together while trying to reconcile the marriage can be included as a part of the required six-month or two-year period, since the law does not wish to discourage people from trying to repair their marriages. There have also been courts that have held that people who are living in the same house, under certain limited circumstances, can be considered to live separate and apart.

The main reason the irreconcilable differences grounds for divorce is not used more frequently is the time requirement. Because people often want to get their divorces as quickly as possible, it is quicker to pursue a divorce based on mental cruelty than to wait for the six-month or two-year time period to elapse.

The words "mental cruelty" can have an impact on the divorce, however. Often spouses who receive a petition for a divorce will be upset that they have been accused of mental cruelty. These hurt feelings can get a case off to a bad start, making a spouse who has been accused of mental cruelty less anxious to reach a reasonable agreement, and wanting to "get back" at the other spouse.

You should discuss with your lawyer the choice of grounds for divorce, and how the impact of the allegations can be reduced. For example, you may wish to discuss with your

20

spouse in advance of filing the petition why you and your attorney have decided to use a particular ground for divorce. This could help to prevent a buildup of negative feelings.

For a discussion of the hearings at which grounds are presented, see Chapter 18.

1.   750 ILCS 5/401.

2.   750 ILCS 5/401(a)(2).

NOTES

CHAPTER 9

DISTRIBUTION OF PROPERTY

One of the functions of a divorce is to divide property between the spouses after their marriage has ended. A divorce order can divide land that people own, and their possessions as well. Often attorneys will refer to these two types of property as real property and personal property. The court can also distribute responsibility for debts.

Some states consider property to be "community property," meaning that upon marriage the property is automatically divided evenly between the spouses, with each receiving one-half of the property. Illinois is not a state that uses a community property system.

In Illinois, property is divided in two ways. First, the court must determine whether property is marital property or nonmarital property.[1] Marital property is a property that is acquired by either spouse or by both spouses during the course of the marriage.

Property that was acquired before the marriage is the nonmarital property of the spouse who had it before the marriage. Also, there are eight exceptions to the general rule that property acquired during the marriage is marital property. Those exceptions are as follows:

1.   property acquired by gift, legacy or descent;

2.   property acquired in exchange for property acquired before the marriage or in exchange for property acquired by gift, legacy or descent;

3.   property acquired by a spouse after a judgment of legal separation;

4.   property excluded by valid agreement of the parties;

5.   any judgment or property obtained by judgment awarded to a spouse from the other spouse;

6.   property acquired before the marriage;

7.   the increase in value of property acquired by a method listed in paragraphs 1 through 6 of this subsection, irrespective of whether the increase results from a contribution of marital property, nonmarital property, the personal effort of a spouse, or

otherwise, subject to the right of reimbursement provided in subsection (c) of this section; and

8. income from property acquired by a method listed in paragraphs 1 through 7 of this subsection if the income is not attributable to the personal effort of a spouse.[2]

The importance of the distinction between marital and nonmarital property is that nonmarital property is awarded to the party who owns it, and marital property can be awarded to either, depending on the facts of the case.

One myth, with regard to property owned by a married couple, is that the title will determine how the property is divided. For example, many people feel that if their name is on the title of a car purchased during marriage, that they will automatically be awarded the car. This is not true. Whether title is held by one spouse or another, if the car was purchased during the marriage, there is a presumption in the law that the car is marital property, and subject to being awarded by the court.

Sometimes the line between marital and nonmarital property is not easy to determine. In some cases, marital and nonmarital property are mixed, as in a commonly held savings account, where one spouse contributes his or her inheritance to that account. Nonmarital property can be changed in this way, referred to as "transmutation," into marital property.[3] It is also possible that one person can be reimbursed for a marital contribution to a nonmarital asset. For example, if a husband owned a house before the marriage, and the couple later added a room to the house, the husband would probably keep the house, and the wife would be given something to reimburse her for her contribution to the extra room. These issues are very complicated, and your lawyer will have to discuss with you how the law applies to your case.

Dividing Marital Property

When the court decides who will get the marital property, it will use the following factors to make its decisions.[4] A judge can consider other factors in addition to these factors:

1. the contribution of each party to the acquisition, preservation, or increase or decrease in value of the marital or nonmarital property, including the contribution of a spouse as a homemaker or to the family unit;

2.   the dissipation of each party of the marital or nonmarital property;

3.   the value of the property assigned to each spouse;

4.   the duration of the marriage;

5.   the relevant economic circumstances of each spouse when the division of property is to become effective, including the desirability of awarding the family home, or the right to live therein for reasonable periods, to the spouse having custody of the children;

6.   any obligations and rights arising from a prior marriage of either party;

7.   any antenuptial agreement of the parties;

8.   the age, health, station, occupation, amount and sources of income, vocational skills, employability, estate, liabilities, and needs of each of the parties;

9.   the custodial provisions for any children;

10.   whether the apportionment is in lieu of or in addition to maintenance;

11.   the reasonable opportunity of each spouse for future acquisition of capital assets and income; and

12.   the tax consequences of the property division upon the respective economic circumstances of the parties.

When a judge decides how to divide property, he or she tries to reach a "just" division. This is frequently referred to as equitable distribution. Equitable does not necessarily mean that each spouse should get half or an equal amount of the property. Many cases reach a result of where one party gets more than half of the property and the other party gets less than half of the property.

The judge is also required to distribute property without consideration of who is at fault in ending the marriage. This means that if one spouse has been proven to be guilty of mental cruelty or adultery or any other grounds for dissolution, the judge cannot consider that as a factor in dividing the property.

There can also be *temporary* orders entered with regard to property. A judge can award temporary support or temporary maintenance (see discussion of maintenance in the following chapter). A judge can order that one party or the other should have possession of certain property while the divorce case is pending. A court can also order one spouse to leave the marital residence if his or her continued presence there would harm the physical or mental health of the other spouse or children.

Another difficult question that often comes up when dividing property is how to consider marital assets that were spent by a spouse during the period when the marriage was breaking up. For example, if the husband takes his new girlfriend on a vacation to Hawaii after the parties have determined that their marriage is over, that should be considered when dividing the remaining property. This kind of spending is referred to as dissipation. In most cases, the court will consider these facts, but you will have to discuss the particular facts of your case with your lawyer to determine whether or not the laws will apply in your case.

Pensions can also be marital property subject to division by a court. Pension plans are often overlooked because they are not an immediately available asset. Rights to a pension, however, can be very important many years down the road. If one spouse has a pension and the other does not, the judge may order a payment to the spouse without a pension at the time of the divorce.

The judge can also enter a qualified domestic relations order, often referred to by its initials, QDRO, to direct a pension plan administrator to distribute pension payments in a certain percentage that the judge determines. In this way, when the spouse who is covered by a pension plan retires, he or she will get a share of the pension, and the former spouse will also get a share. You and your lawyer should also check on how the divorce will affect present or future social security benefits.

Other forms of property can cause problems in determining who should receive what in a divorce. If you or your spouse has received a worker's compensation award or a personal injury award, be sure to bring that to your lawyer's attention so that he or she can determine how those awards will be distributed.

Interests in a business should also be calculated, and often cause problems. If you or your spouse owns a small business, for example, it may be hard to determine the value of the business and what future income you or your spouse can expect from this operation. It is fairly common in these situations to hire an accountant or some other person with special expertise to make assessments with regard to the value of interests in a business.

The value of goodwill in a business can also pose a difficult question for the parties, attorneys, and courts.[5]

Professional degrees can pose problems in a divorce. When one spouse struggles to put another spouse through medical school, for example, the spouse who provided the tuition payments may expect to share in some of the future income of the doctor. Professional degrees may be considered by a court when deciding on the issue of maintenance.

Debts

The beginning of this chapter concerns marital assets, and how some assets can be difficult to distribute upon divorce. While these problems are difficult, there are probably more cases that involve an even less rewarding proposition—assigning debt in a marriage where there are more debts than assets.

While the divorces of millionaires make headlines in newspapers and are reported on TV and radio, the much more typical divorce involves a couple who has some property, and some debts as well. When divorces involve more debts than assets, it is a safe bet that both of the parties will be disappointed with the results of the divorce.

One important fact to keep in mind about debts is that if both parties incurred the debt together, such as a mortgage, a car loan, or a business loan, for which both parties applied, both parties are responsible for that debt, no matter who the judge orders should actually make the payments. For example, if a husband and wife take out a bank loan to purchase a car, the judge may order the husband to make payments, but if the husband later loses his job, is unable to pay, or refuses to pay, the bank will still have the right to pursue collection from the wife. Because of these jointly incurred debts, it is possible that even though the parties may be divorced, they will still have some financial ties to each other.

Finally, one of the debts that may be considered in a divorce case is any debt that a party may owe his or her attorney. It is possible that a judge may order one spouse to pay the other spouse's attorney's fees, or some portion of the attorney's fees.[6] Although this is an option in any case, it is more likely for a court to award attorney's fees where there is a great disparity in the parties' income and assets. In most cases, each party pays his or her own attorney's fees.

1.	750 ILCS 5/503.

2.	750 ILCS 5/503.

3.	750 ILCS 5/503(c).

4.	750 ILCS 5/503(d).

5.	In Re the Marriage of Zells, 143 Ill. 2d 251 (1991).

6.	750 ILCS 5/508.

CHAPTER 10

MAINTENANCE

Maintenance is what used to be referred to as alimony. Sometimes in regular conversation people will still refer to maintenance as alimony, but most judges use the word maintenance. There are no strict guidelines as to when maintenance should be awarded and how much should be awarded. When deciding on the issues of maintenance, a judge is required to consider at least the following 12 factors:[1]

1. the income and property of each party, including marital property assigned to the party seeking maintenance;

2. the needs of each party;

3. the present and future earning capacity of each party;

4. any impairment of the present and future earning capacity of the party seeking maintenance due to that party devoting time to domestic duties or having foregone or delayed education, training, employment, or career opportunities due to the marriage;

5. the time necessary to enable the party seeking maintenance to acquire appropriate education, training, and employment, and whether that party is able to support himself or herself through appropriate employment or is the custodian of a child, making it appropriate that the custodian not seek employment;

6. the standard of living established during the marriage;

7. the duration of the marriage;

8. the age and the physical and emotional condition of both parties;

9. the tax consequences of the property division upon the respective economic circumstances of the parties;

10. contributions and services by the party seeking maintenance to the education, training, career or career potential, or license of the other spouse;

11. any valid agreement of the parties; and

12. any other factor that the court expressly finds to be just and equitable.

From reading the factors that a judge must consider, you can see why maintenance is not awarded in the majority of divorce cases. Since many divorces occur when the husband and wife have not been married long, and are both young, in good physical and emotional condition, and able to earn their own incomes, there are many cases that are not suited to an award of maintenance.

The most frequent kind of case where maintenance is awarded is where the parties have been married for a long time, and one of the spouses, usually the wife, has given up her opportunities for education and employment in order to raise children and assist the husband in his career.

Because one factor that a judge is required to consider when determining a maintenance award is the division of property, decisions on property are usually made first.[2] After the judge has determined who will receive what property, and whether there will be any income available based on the property distribution, the judge can then make a determination with regard to maintenance. Because a judge will consider a case in that order, this is usually how a lawyer will look at decisions regarding maintenance, and how you should be advised as to your rights and obligations in regard to maintenance.

Awards of maintenance can generally be divided into two categories, temporary or rehabilitative, and permanent maintenance. Permanent maintenance is what we frequently think of—a regular payment made by one spouse to the other. Temporary or rehabilitative maintenance is a newer trend that many courts view with favor. This maintenance is either in one lump sum, or in periodic payments for a limited period of time. The theory of temporary or rehabilitative maintenance is that it allows the spouse to seek education or training, and achieve a position of self-sufficiency. Awards of this kind frequently are made for a limited period of time, with the court setting a date to review the facts at a later time. This allows the court to continue the temporary payments if the party receiving payments is doing his or her best job to become self-sufficient, and there is a continuing need.

There are also other circumstances that can end an award of permanent maintenance. Remarriage or living with someone of the opposite sex can mean an end to maintenance. It is possible, however, to reach an agreement in a divorce that can provide for payments to continue even after remarriage. An agreement may also include a provision that the maintenance payments cannot be changed or modified at a future date.

One important note: if you waive your right to maintenance in court, you cannot go back to court to seek it later if you should need it. For example, if both spouses have full-time jobs and they agree that neither should be awarded maintenance, should one spouse later be injured and unable to work, he or she would not be allowed to return to court to seek maintenance from the former spouse.

Because many divorce settlements contain a waiver of maintenance for both sides, it is important that you know and understand what rights and obligations you are waiving. If you have any questions about how a waiver can affect you, be sure to ask your lawyer.

1.	750 ILCS 5/504.

2.	750 ILCS 5/504(a)(1).

NOTES

CHAPTER 11

DOMESTIC VIOLENCE

Violence is present in far too many relationships. Many people who are victims of domestic violence feel that they are alone, and that this kind of situation doesn't happen to other people. After seeking assistance, they are often surprised how common the situation is, and how many people are victims of domestic violence.

Domestic violence does not mean only physical violence, nor does it require bruises or broken bones. The Illinois Domestic Violence Act provides protection to people who are victims of abuse or harassment. Harassment is defined in the Act as any unnecessary conduct which would cause a reasonable person emotional distress.[1]

The law uses specific examples on what would be considered harassment. They include repeated threats of removing the children, following the person around, or repeated phone calls at work. Threats of physical violence can also be harassment.

If you have been a victim of domestic violence, you can obtain assistance through an order of protection. The order can restrain the abuser from any further abuse or harassment, obtain temporary custody of children, provide for temporary visitation schedules, provide temporary child support, and order the abuser to leave the household.

An emergency order of protection can be obtained without having to notify your spouse. This is called an ex parte hearing. An emergency order can last up to 21 days, allowing time for the alleged abuser to be served with the emergency order and the petition for further orders of relief.

An interim order, which lasts longer than an emergency order, can be granted once some notice has been provided to your spouse. A plenary order can last up to two years, and can be renewed at the end of that time if the circumstances allowing renewal are still present. An order of protection can also be incorporated into a divorce, making it a permanent order of protection.

An order of protection can be sought in a divorce, or it can be sought in a separate case, brought either before the divorce or after the divorce is over. The state's attorney's office in your county may also be able to seek an order of protection on your behalf, or use other legal methods to keep your spouse from harming you again.

Domestic violence often occurs in cycles. In the first stage, the victim is on "pins and needles" trying to avoid enraging the abuser. The second stage involves threats or violence. The third stage involves a period when the abuser is remorseful and tries to regain the love and trust of the victim. It is important to keep this cycle of violence in mind when considering filing for an order of protection.

Because of the cyclical nature of domestic violence, it is likely that the abuser will respond by either becoming violent, or by trying to be the super spouse and trying to sweet talk the victim back into the relationship. Because of the potential for violence, no one should rely on a court order for absolute protection. There are cases where a spouse who has been ordered not to abuse or harass the other spouse actually tracks the victim down and kills her.

One place that may be available to assist you if you are a victim is a domestic violence shelter. The shelter can provide emergency housing, and can help in seeking an order of protection. Look for the number in your phone book. Your local police or sheriff's office should also be able to direct you to services that may be available to victims of domestic violence.

The automatic stay that is now in force whenever a summons for dissolution of marriage is filed also offers some protection to people who are victims or potential victims of domestic violence. In any divorce filed in 1993 and thereafter, when the defendant is served with a summons, he or she will get, along with that summons, an automatic provision that prohibits abuse and harassment. Like an order of protection, this automatic stay is not an absolute guarantee, and should not be relied upon to provide safety for you, should you be in fear.

1.   750 ILCS 6/103(6).

CHAPTER 12

PATERNITY

In most marriages, children are conceived and born during the time the parties were married, and there is absolutely no question as to whom the father of the children is. There are some marriages, however, where there are questions involved. For example, a child may have been born during a marriage but conceived before the marriage. It may also happen that a child is conceived and born during the marriage, but the father of the child is not the husband of the marriage. Illinois law provides several ways in which these questions can be resolved.

Illinois law presumes that a child born during the marriage is the child of the husband.[1] If, during the course of the divorce, nobody asserts and proves any facts to the contrary, the court will make a finding that the child is the child of the husband and wife.

In cases where the child was born before the parties were married, paternity can be established by admission of the parties. Both the husband and wife will state in their pleadings that the child was born as a result of the parties' relationship, and the court can then make a finding that the husband is the father of the child.

If there is a dispute over the paternity of a child, there is a fairly easy, although expensive, way to resolve the problem: blood tests. Blood tests, which now involve sampling not only the blood type but also the DNA of the parents, provide a very accurate means of determining whether a particular man is the father of a particular child. Blood samples would have to be taken from the child, the mother, and the man who is alleged to be the father. Because the accuracy of these tests is fairly high, the results are not often challenged.

After paternity has been established, whether by means of a blood test or by admissions of the parties, the determination of which parent should have custody, and what the visitation arrangements should be, would be made the same as in any other divorce case where the child was conceived and born during the marriage. For an explanation of how courts determine custody arrangements, see Chapter 13.

1.   750 ILCS 45/5.

NOTES

CHAPTER 13

CHILD CUSTODY

Dealing with children in a divorce case can be one of the most difficult problems any couple will face. Unlike money or tangible property, children cannot be divided so that a wife may have a certain portion of a child and a husband may have the other portion. A marriage can be ended, but the parent and child relationship will go on.

The decisions are difficult for parents and probably more difficult for courts. Over the years, there have been many changes in how courts deal with custody decisions. Because different custody arrangements are still being evaluated, there are many options that a divorcing couple may wish to consider with regard to child custody.

Sole Custody and Joint Custody

The traditional arrangement in custody matters is for one parent to have what is referred to as "sole custody," meaning that one parent will be responsible for the decision-making with regard to the child, and will have the child with him or her for most of that childhood. When one parent has sole custody, the other parent is entitled to visitation rights. There are some exceptions where, under certain circumstances, visitation will not be granted at all, or will be restricted in some way. See Chapter 14 for discussion of visitation issues.

While sole custody is the traditional choice of families and of courts, there are an increasing number of families choosing joint custody. The court may also impose a joint custody relationship upon a couple. Joint custody means a sharing of both legal and physical custody, but it does not necessarily mean that the child will spend half of his or her time with the mother and the other half with the father. There are many joint custody arrangements where one parent cares for the child for the majority of the time and the other parent has the child on alternate weekends, alternate holidays, and some time over the summer.

One of the main advantages to an award of joint custody is that the decisions about the child's upbringing are not placed solely in one parent's hands. Those decisions must be shared. Decisions about where a child should attend school, what the child's religious training should be, and what kind of medical procedures are needed by the child are made by both parents in a joint custody situation.

Joint custody is often valued by parents who have strong religious beliefs and want to make sure, even if they are not with the child on a daily basis, that they have input into the child's religious upbringing. The use of the words "joint custody" can also have an important psychological impact. Often a parent who would be dissatisfied with visitation rights will be satisfied with a joint custody order because the parent feels that he or she has not given up or "lost" the children.

Joint custody does have its drawbacks. Joint custody requires that the parents work together to resolve disputes that may arise in rearing children. It is likely that parents who are divorcing will have disputes in the future with regard to their children. Illinois law requires a joint parenting order to include a process for resolving disputes. Many couples choose mediation as their method for dispute resolution. Mediation involves a neutral third person who assists the parties in resolving their dispute on their own. For more information about mediation, see Chapter 16 on alternative dispute resolution.

The process of mediation, and further litigation in court if the parties cannot reach an agreement, can be expensive. Those expenses should be considered before deciding on a joint custody arrangement.

What a Judge Considers

When a judge considers which parent should be awarded custody, or whether joint custody is appropriate, the judge must look at what is in the best interest of the child or children. The statute lists seven factors that a judge should consider, among all other relevant factors. Those factors that the court is required to consider are the following:[1]

1.   the wishes of the child's parent or parents as to his custody;
2.   the wishes of the child as to his custodian;
3.   the interaction and interrelationship of the child with his parent or parents, his siblings, and any other person who may significantly affect the child's best interest;
4.   the child's adjustment to his home, school, and community;
5.   the mental and physical health of all individuals involved;

38

6.   the physical violence or threat of physical violence by the child's potential custodian, whether directed against the child or directed against another person; and

7.   the willingness and ability of each parent to facilitate and encourage a close and continuing relationship between the other parent and the child.

Consideration of these factors will be helpful to the judge. In a contested custody case there is rarely a clear-cut answer. The judge is also prohibited from considering any conduct of a parent that does not affect that parent's relationship with the child.[2] For example, one parent may engage in conduct that the other parent feels is irresponsible or immoral. But, as long as that conduct does not affect the child, the court should not consider that conduct when deciding which parent is appropriate for custody. The court is also required to presume that maximum involvement of both parents would be beneficial to the child.[3]

One of the most sticky considerations for any judge, and for parents and lawyers in the preparation of a case, is how to handle the child's wishes. Depending on the age of the child, the child may be called as a witness in the case, or may be asked questions in the judge's office. This is often referred to as an "in camera" interview. In my experience, I have found that judges are well prepared for interviews with children and do their best to put the child at ease.

On the other hand, the situation inevitably involves pressure for the child, and often makes a child feel that he or she is in the position of choosing one parent and hurting the other. If custody will be contested in your case, be sure to talk to your lawyer about the role your child or children will play. It is important to assist your child through the process so that he or she will have the least negative experience that is possible from such a situation.

Probably the most important thing to tell your child is that his or her preference or decision will not guarantee that the judge chooses that arrangement. The judge is required to consider a number of factors, of which your child's preference will only be one. This may help to relieve some of the pressure on a child who will have to testify.

Many years ago, custody decisions were easier because of a rule called the "tender years presumption." According to this rule or guideline, a child under the age of seven

39

would be placed in the custody of the mother. Although you may hear otherwise, mothers and fathers are now on equal footing under the law. But even though the law requires equal treatment, some judges may still have a subtle bias in favor of mothers raising small children. Your lawyer will be familiar with the opinions of judges in your county.

Two issues that can cause problems in custody cases are the religion and race of the parents. When one parent has particularly fervent religious beliefs, that parent may be less likely to allow the other parent to have custody. Joint legal custody may be an appropriate solution to that kind of problem.

If you and your spouse have different religious beliefs, you should be sure to take care to avoid criticizing or ridiculing the other parent's beliefs. Doing so could be a sign to the court that you are not willing and able to encourage a close relationship between your child and the other parent.

The race of the parents and children may also prove to be a difficult issue for the parents and the courts. In one U.S. Supreme Court case, the court decided that a Caucasian mother who divorced and then married an African American man should not be denied custody of her child solely on the basis of her new husband's race.[4] While that court ruling seems clear, there are other cases involving adoption of children that have considered race as a factor when determining an appropriate placement for a child. If race may be an issue in your case, be sure to let your attorney know, so that he or she can prepare adequately to deal with this potentially difficult issue.

Another factor that courts may consider when deciding the appropriate custodial arrangement for children is the relative economic situations of the two parents. It is often the case that, after a divorce, one parent will have a much higher income than the other. While a court may consider these facts, the court will not make a ruling solely on those issues. The person who eventually receives custody of the children will probably receive child support that may help to balance out differences in income. Even a parent with no income can apply for Aid to Families with Dependent Children, so that the children are guaranteed a minimum level of support, including food stamps and health care.

Parents who have a more limited income will have to be more creative to show all concerned that a limited income does not mean limited opportunities for the child or children. For example, a library card can open many opportunities for children at little or no cost. Reading books with your children is also an excellent way to demonstrate your commitment to your child's education and development. The parent with more limited income will also have to be aware that the promise of a new bike or computer game can have a big impact on a child.

The judge in a custody case can also consider psychological evidence with regard to the parents and children. A frequently used concept in these kinds of evaluations is that of "psychological parent." This phrase refers to a theory that in some cases, a child may rely on one parent more than the other for his or her parenting needs. The psychological parent is the parent whom the child would turn to after a bicycle accident, for instance, or when needing instruction on how to do something around the home, or when needing assistance in resolving a dispute with siblings.

A related concept that is often used in custody cases is that of the primary caretaker. Before a divorce, in many households, there is one parent who has primary responsibility for the care of the children, whether that is diapering, taking to the doctor, feeding, bathing, or any of the other tasks associated with raising children. While some states have a presumption that the primary caretaker should be the custodian after divorce, Illinois does not have such a presumption. The theory can be considered by the court, however, in making a decision on custody.

One idea that parents may consider but courts rarely approve is splitting up the children. Although the idea may have some Solomon-style appeal, it is rarely in the best interests of the children. Such an arrangement may make each parent feel like they have not come out a loser, but the children would probably be the losers. The children will suffer enough from the separation from one parent. They should not have to suffer additionally from being separated from siblings.

One other factor to keep in mind when approaching custody decisions is the way in which a custody hearing works. The parties to the custody hearing are the parents, the mother and the father. Each of these parties has an opportunity to be represented by an attorney. Of course, the real people who are concerned with this decision are the children.

The children are not parties to the action, and are rarely represented by an attorney. In some cases, a judge may order that an attorney for the child be involved in a case. That attorney would represent the interests of the child or children.

In other cases, the court may order a slightly different type of attorney, a guardian ad litem, which means guardian for the case. This attorney would represent the best interests of the child to the court. For example, if a child stated a desire to live with one parent, but it was in her best interest to live with the other parent, the guardian ad litem would pursue what was in the child's best interest even if it were different from the child's expressed preference. The parents will usually be required to pay the costs of either the attorney for the child or the guardian ad litem.

When considering custody decisions, it is important not only to know the standard that applies to the decisions—the best interest standard—but what standards are not concerned in a custody case. Frequently, those involved in a custody hearing will talk about one parent or the other being unfit. Unfitness is a different legal standard used by the court when determining whether or not to terminate a person's parental rights, usually in an adoption case. Very few custody cases deal with the issue of fitness, since most parents meet the minimum standards to be fit to retain their parental rights.

Custody orders can also be made on a temporary basis. This may be necessary if the parents cannot reach an agreement as to where the child should stay until the divorce is final. A temporary custody order can also help the parents keep to a schedule of visitation.

Custody orders can be enforced through contacting local law enforcement agencies, either the local police or the sheriff's department. For example, if one parent refuses to return a child after a visitation period, the police or sheriff may be available to accompany the custodial parent to obtain a return of the child. The opposite is also true. A non-custodial parent can seek the help of law enforcement officials to enforce his or her visitation rights.

Because law enforcement officials can provide more effective assistance if the custody order is specific, it is usually advantageous to describe the specific times and dates for custody and visitation exchanges. Without those specifics, it is difficult for the law enforcement officials to determine what the court's order is and to enforce that order.

There are often circumstances where parties want to maintain flexibility. You should keep in mind that if you choose flexibility, you may suffer a corresponding loss in enforceability.

1.   750 ILCS 5/602.

2.   750 ILCS 5/602(b).

3.   750 ILCS 5/602(c).

4.   Palmore v. Sidoti, 466 U.S. 429, 104 S.Ct. 1879, 80 L.Ed. 3d 421.

NOTES

CHAPTER 14

VISITATION

Illinois law presumes that the maximum involvement of both parents is best for their children. The law also requires that visitation for the noncustodial parent not be restricted unless there is serious danger to the child or children.[1] In short, the law requires visitation unless it is a danger to the children.

While the law provides these general guidelines, it does not provide specific examples of what kinds of visitation schedules parents should consider or courts should order. A fairly standard visitation arrangement involves visitation on alternate weekends, alternate holidays, and a longer period of time over the summer.

A visitation plan can be altered to fit the needs of the parents and the children. Specifically, if the noncustodial parent lives a great distance from the custodial parent, families often choose to arrange less frequent but longer periods of visitation.

You may also wish to consider payment for transportation expenses, if travel involves more than driving across town or to the next county. If the transportation involves airfare, be sure to make provisions in a marital settlement agreement, or in the court order, for payment of those costs.

In some families, there may be a need to restrict the visitation of the noncustodial parent, such as where the noncustodial parent is imprisoned, or has a history of committing acts of child abuse. The court can restrict visitation by limiting the time that the noncustodial parent will spend with the child, or by imposing other requirements upon the visitation.

Sometimes the best protection for a child may be that the visitation take place at a location where the custodial parent feels the child will be safe, or that the visitation be supervised by another person who can protect the child.

One of the most frequently asked questions about visitation is whether it is connected to child support. The answer is clearly no. If a parent should lose his or her job and be totally unable to pay any child support, that parent would still have a right to visit the children unless there is a serious danger to the children. This means that even if you believe your former spouse is evading a requirement to pay child support, you cannot deny that person visitation with the children for that reason.

The appropriate avenue for enforcing child support is through the court, not through bargaining over visitation. For more information on child support, see Chapter 15.

Grandparents may also make a request for visitation. If the judge approves, they may be granted specific visitation rights.

1.   750 ILCS 5/607.

CHAPTER 15

CHILD SUPPORT

Child support is an area of the Illinois law that has been steadily improving. It is now easier to calculate the amount of child support that should be paid, and it is now easier to make sure that the child support will be received. But there are still problems. Some of these problems may be resolved in the future with changes in the law. Other problems will most likely remain. And sadly, some children will continue to go unsupported by their noncustodial parents.

The biggest improvement in child support law is the setting of percentage guidelines for payment from the noncustodial parent's income.[1] These guidelines establish a percentage of the parent's net income that should be paid for child support. For example, the noncustodial parent of one child will have to pay 20% of his or her net income for support of that child. The percentage for two children is 25%, for three children 32%. The percentages increase as the number of children increases.

These guidelines are fairly easy to work with if the noncustodial parent has a regular job and a regular paycheck. To determine the net income, the court would exclude any taxes, union dues, payment of child support to other children, and a few other items that are less commonly considered.[2] The problems occur when the noncustodial parent's income changes from week to week or month to month. In that case, what that parent's actual income is may be a subject for debate and for presentation to a judge, if the two parents cannot resolve the issue.

An even more difficult issue is a parent who, for whatever reason, works for cash only, and his or her income cannot be traced or proven. In these cases, it may be possible to prove income by securing the testimony of customers who use this person's service, or by demonstrating the noncustodial parent's average monthly expenditures. If the noncustodial parent is spending $600 a month in rent and utilities, it is fairly easy to conclude that the parent must be earning at least $600 a month from some source.

The other new development that is assisting many Illinois children is automatic withholding of income for child support.[3] This means that when a child support order has been set by a court, the court will enter a separate order, called an order for withholding, which will be sent to the parent's employer. The employer will then withhold the amount that the order for withholding directs and send it directly to the courthouse for distribution to the custodial parent. This makes child support similar to withholding taxes. The noncustodial parent may not like paying, but he or she will never have to transfer the money directly out of the checking account.

Illinois law also protects the noncustodial parent from any kind of retribution by the employer for having to comply with the terms of the order for withholding. This means that an employer cannot choose to fire the employee rather than complete the necessary paperwork for the order for withholding.

There are some situations for which an order for withholding will not work. A noncustodial parent who is receiving Supplemental Security Income (SSI), a Social Security program, cannot have income withheld from that source of payment. U.S. military services, on the other hand, are uniformly cooperative in making sure that necessary child support payments reach the intended child.

Some children may have special needs that require greater support than is allowed by the percentage guidelines. The guidelines are intended to be a minimum so that these special needs can be taken into consideration.[4] Be sure to inform your attorney if your child or children have any special needs, particularly medical or schooling needs that are expensive. The law also makes a special provision for providing for disabled children even after they have reached the age of 18,[5] when child support normally ends. It is important to bring your child's disabilities to the attention of your lawyer so that an appropriate support award can be pursued.

Illinois law also provides for the possibility that noncustodial parents may have to contribute to the educational expenses of their children even after the children have reached the age of 18. This kind of child support is not automatically granted. It must be set by a court order. The court will consider the income of both parents before determining whether a noncustodial parent has an obligation to pay for any part of the child's education after age 18.

Some choose to make arrangements for post-majority support in the context of their divorce, and others choose to have the issue reserved. That means that the judge will decide later if either party asks the judge to do so.

Child support orders can also be made on a temporary basis. Temporary orders may be necessary if the person who has the child or children is unable to support those children until the divorce is finally resolved. A temporary support order can be made by an agreement, which would be presented to a judge, or after a contested hearing if the parents cannot agree.

1.   750 ILCS 5/505(1).

2.   750 ILCS 5/505(3).

3.   750 ILCS 5/706.1.

4.   750 ILCS 5/505(2).

5.   750 ILCS 5/513.

NOTES

CHAPTER 16
ALTERNATIVE DISPUTE RESOLUTION

People are often disappointed at the process they must go through to obtain a divorce. That process is a fundamental part of our legal heritage—the adversarial system. The adversarial system is one in which attorneys represent people with different interests. Each attorney has an obligation to advocate for the interests of his or her client.

The adversarial system can produce conflicts where none existed before. For example, suppose a husband and wife decide to get a divorce and decide how they wish to divide the property and what arrangements should be made for child custody. Each of the spouses then goes to an attorney for advice on the agreement. The attorney has the obligation to tell the client whether he or she may get a better deal by going to court rather than agreeing to the proposed settlement.

Depending on what the clients choose, a divorce may start out as a peaceful and cooperative agreement and end in a hard fought legal battle in court. Many divorced people, attorneys, and judges have realized that this adversarial system may not be the best way to resolve problems, particularly in cases where there are children and the parents will need to cooperate to some degree as long as the children are minors.

In recognition of the problems of the adversarial system, some counties have initiated programs to make the divorce experience a more positive and cooperative one. In general, these programs are lumped into the category of "alternative dispute resolution."

The most frequently used alternative method is that of mediation. Mediation is a process where a neutral third person assists the two parties in reaching an agreement, if any agreement can be reached. The mediator assists each party in explaining their perspective of the dispute to the other, and assists them in listening to each other, something that does not always happen easily in the midst of a divorce. With the assistance of the mediator, the parties try to develop possible solutions to their problems. The mediation may result in an agreement, which can be put into writing by the parties' attorneys, and approved by the court. Of course, no alternative program will be totally successful.

Many who engage in mediation will not reach an agreement and will continue with the divorce process through a court. If an agreement is reached, however, the parties may be spared some of the ill feelings that can develop in a contested hearing. The mediation process is also one that can be used if disputes come up after the divorce.

The state legislature has decided alternative dispute resolution is essential in cases where parents agree or are ordered to have joint custody of children. Each joint custody order must contain a description of the process the parties will use to resolve disputes that they may have in the future about their children.[1]

Mediators come in all varieties. Many people may already use a mediation style process without labeling it that way. Couples may turn to a pastor, a rabbi, or other spiritual leader for assistance in resolving a dispute that they cannot resolve themselves. Sometimes family members fill the same role. When both the husband and wife trust a particular parent, aunt, uncle, or friend, they may turn to that person for assistance in resolving a dispute. Formal mediation may require more training.

In some counties where courts order couples to engage in mediation before they can proceed with a contested divorce, the court rules require selection of a trained mediator. Training can help a mediator learn how to avoid escalating tensions in a mediation session. Training can also help a mediator identify situations where mediation is not appropriate. For example, if it is clear that one spouse is exercising undue control over the other spouse, mediation will not produce a meaningful agreement and should be suspended. For this reason, in families where there has been domestic violence, mediation may be inappropriate.

One other method of alternative dispute resolution that is less often used in family law is that of arbitration. Arbitration is different from mediation in that the arbitrator, not the couple, makes the decision. Arbitration is similar to having a judge decide a dispute. Arbitration can often speed the process of resolving a dispute, and can also reduce the costs. As with mediators, it is wise to know the qualifications of an arbitrator before selecting one.

A final program that many counties require is called the Children First program. The program includes a series of videotapes and discussions about situations in which children are caught in the middle of divorcing or divorced parents. Each parent attends the sessions separately from the other parent. The aim of this program is to educate parents about the impact of divorce on children, and to help parents reduce the negative impact of divorce on their children. It has been my experience that this program is most helpful when parties are so consumed by the dispute with their spouse that they fail to realize the impact the dispute is having on the children.

All of these alternative dispute resolution methods differ from county to county. Your attorney is the best person to consult about which methods, if any, are required in your area.

1.   750 ILCS 5/602.1(b).

NOTES

CHAPTER 17
DISCOVERY

In everyday language, a discovery is something that is new and exciting and different. In the context of a divorce, discovery probably won't be too exciting, but it is an important part of a case. In law, discovery refers to a variety of methods that can be used to obtain information about a case. Informal discovery is very common. For example, your lawyer may call your spouse's attorney to find out information about income or debts, or to ask for certain documents.

Formal discovery is a set of procedures established by law to help parties obtain information. The laws on discovery also provide for penalties if someone does not comply with the discovery requests.

Interrogatories are a frequently used method of discovery. Interrogatories are lists of questions submitted by one party to the other party. The questions must be answered in writing and under oath. If you receive interrogatories, your attorney will probably give you a copy of the questions and ask you to draft answers to those questions. Your attorney will probably then review your answers with you to make sure that the questions have been answered completely.

Often interrogatories will ask questions about items that have not been involved in your marriage. For example, your attorney may send out interrogatories to your spouse asking whether he or she owns any stocks or bonds, has rights to a pension, or has other investments. Sometimes interrogatories are used in this way to help narrow the focus of a case and to rule out issues not involved.

Another form of written discovery is the request to produce. A request to produce is a written list of documents or other tangible things that one attorney asks the other to produce either for inspection or copying. Requests to produce may be used to obtain bank records, property records, and other written records related to marital finances.

Depositions are a more lively form of discovery. In depositions, the parties or other witnesses can be made to be present for questioning. This questioning is similar to the questioning that may occur in court if a hearing is necessary, but questions may be more broad. The persons answering the questions are required to testify under oath.

Depositions are more useful for questions that need to be explored in detail. For example, in custody cases where a parent's use of discipline may be questioned, a deposition allows an attorney to probe more deeply and ask follow-up questions to any answers that are incomplete or that suggest other questions to be asked.

Some divorce cases that involve custody may also involve examinations of the parties. This happens most frequently when one or more parties ask for a psychologist to evaluate themselves or the child or children.[1] The court may also order that a "home study" be completed.[2] A home study involves a neutral person, usually from a social service agency, inspecting the homes of each of the parties to make sure that they are suitable for the children.

There are also special discovery rules that apply to expert witnesses. For example, if you and your attorney decide to hire a psychologist to testify about child custody, there are special rules that apply to notifying the other side about the existence of your expert witness, and to what he or she plans to testify. The rules for who can be an expert witness and when advance notice is required are fairly complicated. If you have been considering the use of an expert witness, be sure to notify your attorney right away so that he or she can determine what rules apply to disclosure of the expert.

1. 750 ILCS 5/604.

2. 750 ILCS 5/605.

CHAPTER 18
HEARINGS

Of all the parts of the process of obtaining a divorce, the hearing can be the most tension filled. Even in cases where all the issues have been resolved and the parties have agreed on the settlement, a hearing can make people nervous. The experience is somewhat like driving by a police officer even when you are not speeding. It seems that an automatic reaction is to take your foot off the accelerator, put your foot on the brakes, and check your speedometer. You have done nothing wrong, but you feel nervous nonetheless.

Illinois law provides for divorces to be held in two separate stages. The first stage is a hearing on grounds for the divorce. The second stage is when all other issues can be considered. This arrangement is made so that the issues of grounds, which are in no way related to the other issues, do not affect the parties or the judge when considering the remaining issues of the divorce. When parties reach an agreement early on in the divorce process, it is common to combine the two hearings into one, so that only one court appearance is necessary.

In a first-stage hearing, the hearing on grounds, it is typical that only one of the spouses will testify. If you are the spouse who will be testifying, your lawyer will explain to you the questions that will be asked of you during the hearing. The other side will have an opportunity to question you on grounds, but usually this is not contested. In the second stage of the divorce, the hearings are much more like the courtroom dramas that we see on TV. One lawyer calls a witness, the other lawyer will have an opportunity to cross-examine.

One factor that can complicate a hearing is if one of the parties is representing himself or herself. The phrase used to describe this is "pro se," meaning "for yourself." The party who is without a lawyer probably will not know exactly how the hearing will work, and may cause some changes in what otherwise would be a routine hearing.

The judge is usually in an awkward position when someone is representing himself or herself. The judge cannot be an attorney for the person who does not have one, but at the same time the judge does not want to have one person put at an unfair disadvantage.

One problem with pro se parties is that they frequently try to introduce evidence or ask questions about matters that are wholly unrelated to the proceeding. Often this is done from bitterness over the end of the relationship. Although the lawyer would object to such questions, there is no way to avoid the hard feelings that are brought out when one spouse tries to use a hearing as one last shot to irritate his or her spouse.

Default hearings, where the other spouse has opted not to participate, are the easiest. Default means that the spouse was served with the petition and the summons for the divorce, and did not respond within the time allowed. In these cases, the spouse is usually not present at the hearing, and the party who filed the suit, along with his or her lawyer, will have a fairly easy task of explaining to the judge the issues involved, and how they are asking the judge to resolve those issues. The judge will not automatically accept any order proposed in a case where one party is in default, but it is obviously less of a burden when there is no one to argue on the other side.

Divorces where the parties have agreed to all the terms of the settlement are also fairly easy. Depending on the judge, he or she may ask for testimony about how the parties have decided to resolve the issues. At times, the judge may simply review the settlement agreement and sign the order.

One annoying problem with divorces in Illinois is the lack of privacy. There is no rule that automatically requires other people to leave the courtroom during a divorce case. In fact, courts frequently will schedule time periods when many uncontested divorces will be heard at the same time. This means that several individuals or couples will all be waiting in the courtroom for their cases to be called. The result is often that people must testify about the grounds of their divorce in a room full of strangers also obtaining divorces. Probably the best way to avoid letting this situation bother you is to concentrate strictly on the judge and your lawyer.

Contested hearings involve a great deal of preparation. Make sure that you discuss with your attorney any specific strategies he or she may have on answering questions that are posed to you at the hearing.

One basic rule is to make sure that you listen carefully to the question that is asked so that you answer the question precisely. Also, sometimes it is hard to remember that although you know the facts involved in your case backwards and forwards, the judge is probably hearing these facts for the first time. This means that you will have to testify to some basic things, like the fact that you were married, your children's names and ages, where you live, and where your children go to school.

You should also discuss with your attorney any particular strategies that he or she may have about answering questions that may be objectionable. For example, I usually advise my clients that if they feel uncomfortable with a question, they should take a deep breath before answering. This will frequently be enough time to give me the opportunity to make an objection to the question so that the judge can rule on whether or not the question should be answered before the answer has actually come out of my client's mouth.

If children are involved, it is possible that the children may be asked to serve as witnesses or testify in the judge's office. If your children need to be present, make sure to have a baby sitter or other relative who can be responsible for handling the children while you are in the courtroom.

Another frequently asked question about hearings is what clothes are appropriate. Since judges can be very particular about what is worn in their courtroom, you should avoid items like blue jeans, tank tops, baseball caps, and revealing clothes. You may also want to consult with your lawyer about any particular issues like beards, earrings, or any other clothing or decoration that you wear that may be unusual.

NOTES

CHAPTER 19
RESOURCES

Any divorce, even one that is "uncontested," can be a difficult experience. It involves a major change in a person's life. You have the assistance of an attorney for your legal needs, but you may have other needs for which your attorney is not as well suited. One of the first places I turn to when I need information is the library. Whether you are concerned about how your children will deal with divorce, or are considering the stresses of remarriage, your local library will have books to help you, or will be able to get those books through interlibrary loans. You may want to start by requesting some of the books listed in Appendix B of this book.

If you prefer to seek help from people rather than books, there are several places to which you can turn. Mental health agencies, social services agencies, religious counselors, and support groups all offer different assistance to people who are experiencing a stressful divorce.

Local mental health agencies are equipped to provide counseling and other similar services to you as an individual, and to your children if necessary. You can contact your local mental health agency for more information about what services they provide, what the cost would be, and whether there is any waiting list to receive such services. You will probably find that the agencies provide outstanding service, limited by the small amount of funds they receive to help them provide services.

There are also various social services agencies, both public and private, which may be able to provide assistance to you. The Illinois Department of Children and Family Services (DCFS), which has regional and local offices throughout the state, can provide some assistance if you have problems related to your children. For example, DCFS provides a program called Project Twelve Ways which focuses on parenting skills. You may find the extra support helpful in a situation where you are assuming new responsibilities with regard to your children. Other private agencies, such as Lutheran Social Services of Illinois or Catholic Social Services, may provide many of the same services and more.

Many psychologists work in private practice and are not associated with any particular agency. They are listed in the phone directory under psychologists and counselors. Your lawyer may also be able to recommend a psychologist to you.

You may choose to find help from people who are going through or have been through the same stresses that you are experiencing. Support groups provide some confirmation that you are not the only person who has had difficulties with these issues. They also provide a fairly constructive way to release some of the tensions involved in a divorce. A support group can be as informal as an irregular lunch with friends of yours who are divorced or divorcing. There may also be support groups organized by mental health agencies, social service agencies, your church or synagogue, or a local university.

Your lawyer may have ideas or suggestions that are unique to your area, so if you need assistance, be sure to ask your lawyer as well.

CHAPTER 20

AFTER THE DIVORCE

After the divorce order has been granted, you will probably feel a great sense of relief that the process is finally over. There are circumstances, however, where having a final divorce order does not mean that your involvement with your former spouse is complete, and does not end the work that must be done. If you have children, or if you have financial assets or liabilities that are still tied to your former spouse, you will probably have some continuing contact with either your former spouse or his or her attorney.

If you have children, the children will ordinarily spend time with each parent, depending on the court's order for custody and visitation. Problems can come up when parents' or children's schedules change or when families move farther apart than they were when the divorce was granted. If you experience problems in obtaining your child for either a custodial or visitation period, you can seek help from one of two sources. Law enforcement officials may be used to enforce an order that is specific enough to show them that the court has ordered a child to be with a particular parent at a certain time.

If the order is not specific enough, you can seek relief from the court that granted the divorce order. There is a specific law on the process for enforcing visitation rights. A court order may also be enforced by seeking to have the offending person held in contempt, meaning that the court would punish the other party for not living up to his or her part of the divorce order.

If the problem is collecting child support, you may work through your attorney, or you may also work through attorneys provided through a combination of state and federal laws to enforce child support orders. In some parts of Illinois, this function is handled by the state's attorney. In other parts of the state, this function is handled by the Illinois Attorney General's Bureau of Child Support Enforcement. These lawyers can also work with their counterparts in other states if the parent who owes support has moved.

There may also be times when you need to change the divorce order for one reason or other. A change in an order is usually referred to as a modification. Not all aspects of a divorce order can be modified, but those aspects dealing particularly with children are modifiable.

Custody orders can be changed. Custody can be moved from one parent to another, or joint custody established or ended. In general, the law requires that to change custody more than two years after the most recent custody order, you must show the court that there has been a change in circumstances and that a change in custody is necessary for the child's best interest.[1]

If you want to change custody sooner than two years after the last order, you must be able to prove to the court that your child is in serious danger, and that a change in custody is necessary for his or her best interests.[2] Changing custody when there is a joint parenting order has slightly different standards, which you may want to discuss with your attorney if you have a joint parenting agreement.

Child support may also need to be changed from time to time. If a child's needs increase, or if the noncustodial parent's income substantially increases, you may wish to consider returning to court to obtain an increased amount of child support.

Probably the most important time to return to court in terms of child support is if you are the parent who is paying support and you have either lost a job or suffered a substantial decrease in income. Even if your former spouse is understanding and does not complain about a lack of child support when you are unemployed, it is important to return to court to have your obligation changed by a court order. That court order is necessary because until the support amount is reduced, you will continue to build up overdue payments every month.

Even when both parents agree that support payments should be reduced for some period of time, it is important for the parent who is paying child support to have that agreement reflected in the court order.

Maintenance, what used to be called alimony, can also be modified under some circumstances, if it was awarded in the initial divorce decree. If neither party is awarded maintenance in the initial divorce decree, neither party can seek maintenance later. On the other hand, if one person is awarded maintenance, there may be circumstances where that amount of maintenance can be adjusted in the future.

Sometimes a court will set a schedule for that adjustment, stating in its order that maintenance will last for a certain number of years and then be reviewed by the court. Even maintenance awards that are not specifically slated to be reviewed by the court may be reviewed if there is a substantial change in circumstances of the parties, particularly income.

One other change that parties may contemplate after a divorce is moving to another state. While families who are married do not need permission from any court to move from one state to another, a parent who has custody of his or her children must seek permission of the court before he or she moves from the state of Illinois.[3] Illinois calls this removal.

Removal used to be fairly routine if the custodial parent had a new job in a new state, was transferred to a new state, or had a new spouse that had a job change. A fairly recent Illinois Supreme Court case has changed how judges must view these circumstances, and has made it more difficult to obtain permission to leave the state of Illinois.[4] The court must consider what benefit there would be to the child for the move, what relationship the child has with his or her noncustodial parent, and whether a reasonable visitation schedule could be arranged after the move. These are important factors for both parents to keep in mind when the custodial parent is considering a move outside of Illinois.

Divorce can also have effects on many government benefits. Some Social Security benefits, for example, can be based on a spouse's income, and those benefits will be awarded to a former spouse only if the marriage has been long enough to qualify. The Social Security office may need a certified copy of your divorce order to make sure that benefits are awarded properly.

Military pension benefits can also be affected by divorce. A former spouse can receive part of a military spouse's pension only if certain forms are completed, and completed at the right time. With these benefits, it is important to remember that a court order alone may not be enough to affect pension benefits paid to a former spouse. You may wish to check, or have your attorney check, with a military officer who is familiar with pension requirements. There are also organizations that may be able to assist you in making sure that military pension benefits are appropriately distributed.

Public aid benefits, also known as aid to families with dependent children, or AFDC, can also be affected by divorce. If a parent is receiving a grant for children in his or her care, that parent should make sure, if there is a joint custody relationship, that the parent who wishes to maintain the public aid grant should have the children at least 51% of the time. If one parent does not have the children more than half the time, you could be putting at risk the children's grant, and probably more important, their status as recipients of medical cards.

Taxes can also keep divorced parents communicating long after the divorce. If the divorce decree does not make it clear who is entitled to claim children as a tax exemption, it can be a point of contention between parents. The best way to resolve that issue is to consult with a tax accountant who can advise both parents in a neutral manner as to what tax requirements are and what the liabilities would be. Often these families will find that they can arrange their taxes to either maximize the return or minimize a payment of taxes.

Unfortunately, bankruptcy is also a consideration that many people face after a divorce. Bankruptcy can absolve people of some debts, but not all. Child support payments, including overdue payments, cannot be compromised, and maintenance payments cannot be revised through bankruptcy. On the other hand, if one spouse is making a regular payment to his or her former spouse by way of a property settlement, this debt could potentially be discharged in bankruptcy.

Bankruptcy can also have an impact on jointly held debts to third parties. For example, a husband and wife agree in their divorce settlement that the husband will be responsible for credit card debts that were incurred jointly during the marriage. If the husband should later file for bankruptcy, he could have his responsibility discharged, and the credit card company would be able to pursue the wife.

After a divorce, you may also wish to consider making a will, or revising a will that you made previously. If you do not revise a will that includes a former spouse who would receive part of your belongings, the former spouse is automatically excluded from receiving any portion of your estate. On the other hand, you may have specific items that you had designated to be received by your former spouse or relative. After a divorce, you may want to review whether or not your property should be distributed in the same manner.

1.   750 ILCS 5/610(b).

2.   750 ILCS 5/610(a).

3.   750 ILCS 5/609.

4.   In Re the Marriage of Eckert, 119 Ill. 2d 316, 116 Ill. Dec. 220, 518 N.E. 2d 1041.

NOTES

ILLINOIS STATUTES 750 ILCS

PART IV—DISSOLUTION AND LEGAL SEPARATION

5/401. Dissolution of marriage

§ 401. Dissolution of marriage. (a) The court shall enter a judgment of dissolution of marriage if at the time the action was commenced one of the spouses was a resident of this State or was stationed in this State while a member of the armed services, and the residence or military presence had been maintained for 90 days next preceding the commencement of the action or the making of the finding; provided, however, that a finding of residence of a party in any judgment entered under this Act from January 1, 1982 through June 30, 1982 shali satisfy the former domicile requirements of this Act; and if one of the following grounds for dissolution has been proved:

(1) That, without cause or provocation by the petitioner: the respondent was at the time of such marriage, and continues to be naturally impotent; the respondent had a wife or husband living at the time of the marriage; the respondent had committed adultery subsequent to the marriage; the respondent has wilfully deserted or absented himself or herself from the petitioner for the space of one year, including any period during which litigation may have pended between the spouses for dissolution of marriage or legal separation; the respondent has been guilty of habitual drunkenness for the space of 2 years; the respondent has been guilty of gross and confirmed habits caused by the excessive use of addictive drugs for the space of 2 years, or has attempted the life of the other by poison or other means showing malice, or has been guilty of extreme and repeated physical or mental cruelty, or has been convicted of a felony or other infamous crime; or the respondent has infected the other with a communicable venereal disease. "Excessive use of addictive drugs", as used in this Section, refers to use of an addictive drug by a person when using the drug becomes a controlling or a dominant purpose of his life; or

(2) That the spouses have lived separate and apart for a continuous period in excess of 2 years and irreconcilable differences have caused the irretrievable breakdown of the marriage and the court determines that efforts at reconciliation have failed or that future attempts at reconciliation would be impracticable and not in the best interests of the family. If the spouses have lived separate and apart for a continuous period of not less than 6 months next preceding the entry of the judgment dissolving the marriage, as evidenced by testimony or affidavits of the spouses, the requirement of living separate and apart for a continuous period in excess of 2 years may be waived upon written stipulation of both spouses filed with the court. At any time after the parties cease to cohabit, the following periods shall be included in the period of separation:

(A) any period of cohabitation during which the parties attempted in good faith to reconcile and participated in marriage counseling under the guidance of any of the following: a psychiatrist, a clinical psychologist, a clinical social worker, a marriage and family therapist, a person authorized to provide counseling in accordance with the prescriptions of any religious denomination, or a person regularly engaged in providing family or marriage counseling; and

(B) any period of cohabitation under written agreement of the parties to attempt to reconcile.

PART V—PROPERTY, SUPPORT AND ATTORNEY FEES

5/503. Disposition of property

§ 503. Disposition of property. (a) For purposes of this Act, "marital property" means all property acquired by either spouse subsequent to the marriage, except the following, which is known as "non-marital property":

(1) property acquired by gift, legacy or descent;

(2) property acquired in exchange for property acquired before the marriage or in exchange for property acquired by gift, legacy or descent;

(3) property acquired by a spouse after a judgment of legal separation;

(4) property excluded by valid agreement of the parties;

(5) any judgment or property obtained by judgment awarded to a spouse from the other spouse;

(6) property acquired before the marriage;

(7) the increase in value of property acquired by a method listed in paragraphs (1) through (6) of this subsection, irrespective of whether the increase results from a contribution of marital property, non-marital property, the personal effort of a spouse, or otherwise, subject to the right of reimbursement provided in subsection (c) of this Section; and

(8) income from property acquired by a method listed in paragraphs (1) through (7) of this subsection if the income is not attributable to the personal effort of a spouse.

(b) For purposes of distribution of property pursuant to this Section, all property acquired by either spouse after the marriage and before a judgment of dissolution of marriage or declaration of invalidity of marriage, including non-marital property transferred into some form of co-ownership between the spouses, is presumed to be marital property, regardless of whether title is held individually or by the spouses in some form of co-ownership such as joint tenancy, tenancy in common, tenancy by the entirety, or community property. The presumption of marital property is overcome by a showing that the property was acquired by a method listed in subsection (a) of this Section.

(c) Commingled marital and non-marital property shall be treated in the following manner, unless otherwise agreed by the spouses:

(1) When marital and non-marital property are commingled by contributing one estate of property into another resulting in a loss of identity of the contributed property, the classification of the contributed property is transmuted to the estate receiving the contribution, subject to the provisions of paragraph (2) of this subsection; provided that if marital and non-marital property are commingled into newly acquired property resulting in a loss of identity of the contributing estates, the commingled property shall be deemed transmuted to marital property, subject to the provisions of paragraph (2) of this subsection.

(2) When one estate of property makes a contribution to another estate of property, or when a spouse contributes personal effort to non-marital property, the contributing estate shall be reimbursed from the estate receiving the contribution notwithstanding any transmutation; provided, that no such reimbursement shall be made with respect to a contribution which is not retraceable by clear and convincing evidence, or was a gift, or , in the case of a contribution of personal effort of a spouse to non-marital property, unless the effort is significant and results in substantial appreciation of the non-marital property. Personal effort of a spouse shall be deemed a contribution by the marital estate. The court may provide for reimbursement out of the marital property to be divided or by imposing a lien against the non-marital property which received the contribution.

(d) In a proceeding for dissolution of marriage or declaration of invalidity of marriage, or in a proceeding for disposition of property following dissolution of marriage by a court which lacked personal jurisdiction over the absent spouse or lacked jurisdiction to dispose of the property, the court shall assign each spouse's non-marital property to that spouse. It also shall divide the marital property without regard to marital misconduct in just proportions considering all relevant factors, including:

(1) the contribution of each party to the acquisition, preservation, or increase or decrease in value of the marital or non-marital property, including the contribution of a spouse as a homemaker or to the family unit;

(2) the dissipation by each party of the marital or non-marital property;

(3) the value of the property assigned to each spouse;

(4) the duration of the marriage;

(5) the relevant economic circumstances of each spouse when the division of property is to become effective, including the desirability of awarding the family home, or the right to live therein for reasonable periods, to the spouse having custody of the children;

(6) any obligations and rights arising from a prior marriage of either party;

(7) any antenuptial agreement of the parties;

(8) the age, health, station, occupation, amount and sources of income, vocational skills, employability, estate, liabilities, and needs of each of the parties;

(9) the custodial provisions for any children;

(10) whether the apportionment is in lieu of or in addition to maintenance;

(11) the reasonable opportunity of each spouse for future acquisition of capital assets and income; and

(12) the tax consequences of the property division upon the respective economic circumstances of the parties.

(e) Each spouse has a species of common ownership in the marital property which vests at the time dissolution proceedings are commenced and continues only during the pendency of the action. Any such interest in marital property shall not encumber that property so as to restrict its transfer, assignment or conveyance by the title holder unless such title holder is specifically enjoined from making such transfer, assignment or conveyance.

(f) In a proceeding for dissolution of marriage or declaration of invalidity of marriage or in a proceeding for disposition of property following dissolution of marriage by a court that lacked personal jurisdiction over the absent spouse or lacked jurisdiction to dispose of the property, the court, in determining the value of the marital and non-marital property for purposes of dividing the property, shall value the property as of the date of trial or some other date as close to the date of trial as is practicable.

(g) The court if necessary to protect and promote the best interests of the children may set aside a portion of the jointly or separately held estates of the parties in a separate fund or trust for the support, maintenance, education, and general welfare of any minor, dependent, or incompetent child of the parties. In making a determination under this subsection, the court may consider, among other things, the conviction of a party of any of the offenses set forth in Section 12-4, 12-4.1, 12-4.2, 12-4.3, 12-13, 12-14, 12-15, or 12-16 of the Criminal Code of 1961[1] if the victim is a child of one or both of the parties, and there is a need for, and cost of, care, healing and counseling for the child who is the victim of the crime.

(h) Unless specifically directed by a reviewing court, or upon good cause shown, the court shall not on remand consider any increase or decrease in the value of any "marital" or "non-marital" property occurring since the assessment of such property at the original trial or hearing, but shall use only that assessment made at the original trial or hearing.

(i) The court may make such judgments affecting the marital property as may be just and may enforce such judgments by ordering a sale of marital property, with proceeds therefrom to be applied as determined by the court.

5/504. Maintenance

§ 504. Maintenance. (a) In a proceeding for dissolution of marriage or legal separation or declaration of invalidity of marriage, or a proceeding for maintenance following dissolution of the marriage by a court which lacked personal jurisdiction over the absent spouse, the court may grant a temporary or permanent maintenance award for either spouse in amounts and for periods of time as the court deems just, without regard to marital misconduct, in gross or for fixed or indefinite periods of time, and the maintenance may be paid from the income or property of the other spouse after consideration of all relevant factors, including:

(1) the income and property of each party, including marital property apportioned and non-marital property assigned to the party seeking maintenance;

(2) the needs of each party;

(3) the present and future earning capacity of each party;

(4) any impairment of the present and future earning capacity of the party seeking maintenance due to that party devoting time to domestic duties or having foregone or delayed education, training, employment, or career opportunities due to the marriage;

(5) the time necessary to enable the party seeking maintenance to acquire appropriate education, training, and employment, and whether that party is able to support himself or herself through appropriate employment or is the custodian of a child making it appropriate that the custodian not seek employment;

(6) the standard of living established during the marriage;

(7) the duration of the marriage;

(8) the age and the physical and emotional condition of both parties;

(9) the tax consequences of the property division upon the respective economic circumstances of the parties;

(10) contributions and services by the party seeking maintenance to the education, training, career or career potential, or license of the other spouse;

(11) any valid agreement of the parties; and

(12) any other factor that the court expressly finds to be just and equitable.

5/505. Child support—Contempt—Penalties

§ 505. Child Support; Contempt; Penalties. (a) In a proceeding for dissolution of marriage, legal separation, declaration of invalidity of marriage, a proceeding for child support following dissolution of the marriage by a court which lacked personal jurisdiction over the absent spouse, a proceeding for modification of a previous order for child support under Section 510 of this Act, or any proceeding authorized under Section 501 or 601 of this Act, the court may order either or both parents owing a duty of support to a child of the marriage to pay an amount reasonable and necessary for his support, without regard to marital misconduct. The duty of support owed to a minor child includes the obligation to provide for the reasonable and necessary physical, mental and emotional health needs of the child.

(1) The Court shall determine the minimum amount of support by using the following guidelines:

Number of Children	Percent of Supporting Party's Net Income
1	20%
2	25%
3	32%
4	40%
5	45%
6 or more	50%

(2) The above guidelines shall be applied in each case unless the court, after considering evidence presented on all relevant factors, finds a reason for deviating from the guidelines. Relevant factors may include but are not limited to:

(a) the financial resources of the child;

(b) the financial resources and needs of the custodial parent;

(c) the standard of living the child would have enjoyed had the marriage not been dissolved;

(d) the physical and emotional condition of the child, and his educational needs; and

(e) the financial resources and needs of the non-custodial parent.

If the court deviates from the guidelines, based on consideration of the factors in paragraphs (2)(a) through (2)(e) of subsection (a) of this Section, or any other relevant factor, it shall make express findings as to its reason for doing so.

(3) "Net income" is defined as the total of all income from all sources, minus the following deductions:

(a) Federal income tax (properly calculated withholding or estimated payments);

(b) State income tax (properly calculated withholding or estimated payments);

(c) Social Security (FICA payments);

(d) Mandatory retirement contributions required by law or as a condition of employment;

(e) Union dues;

(f) Dependent and individual health/hospitalization insurance premiums;

(g) Prior obligations of support or maintenance actually paid pursuant to a court order;

(h) Expenditures for repayment of debts that represent reasonable and necessary expenses for the production of income, medical expenditures necessary to preserve life or health, reasonable expenditures for the benefit of the child and the other parent, exclusive of gifts. The court shall reduce net income in determining the minimum amount of support to be ordered only for the period that such payments are due and shall enter an order containing provisions for its self-executing modification upon termination of such payment period.

(4) In cases where the court order provides for health/hospitalization insurance coverage pursuant to Section 505.2 of this Act, the premiums for that insurance, or that portion of the premiums for which the supporting party is responsible in the case of

insurance provided through an employer's health insurance plan where the employer pays a portion of the premiums, shall be subtracted from net income in determining the minimum amount of support to be ordered.

(5) If the net income cannot be determined because of default or any other reason, the court shall order support in an amount considered reasonable in the particular case. The final order in all cases shall state the support level in dollar amounts.

(b) Failure of either parent to comply with an order to pay support shall be punishable as in other cases of contempt. In addition to other penalties provided by law the Court may, after finding the parent guilty of contempt, order that the parent be:

(1) placed on probation with such conditions of probation as the Court deems advisable;

(2) sentenced to periodic imprisonment for a period not to exceed 6 months; provided, however, that the Court may permit the parent to be released for periods of time during the day or night to:

(A) work; or

(B) conduct a business or other self-employed occupation.

The Court may further order any part or all of the earnings of a parent during a sentence of periodic imprisonment paid to the Clerk of the Circuit Court or to the parent having custody or to the guardian having custody of the minor children of the sentenced parent for the support of said minor children until further order of the Court.

5/505.2. Health insurance

§ 505.2. Health insurance. (a) Definitions. As used in this Section:

(1) "Obligee" means the individual to whom the duty of support is owed or the individual's legal representative.

(2) "Obligor" means the individual who owes a duty of support pursuant to an order for support.

(3) "Public office" means any elected official or any State or local agency which is or may become responsible by law for enforcement of, or which is or may become authorized to enforce, an order for support, including, but not limited to: the Attorney General, the Illinois Department of Public Aid, the Illinois Department of Mental Health and Developmental Disabilities, the Illinois Department of Children and Family Services,

and the various State's Attorneys, Clerks of the Circuit Court and supervisors of general assistance.

(b) Order. Whenever the court establishes, modifies or enforces an order for child support or for child support and maintenance the court shall, upon request of the obligee or Public Office, order that any child covered by the order be named as a beneficiary of any health insurance plan that is available to the obligor through an employer or labor union or trade union. If the court finds that such a plan is not available to the obligor, or that the plan is not accessible to the obligee, the court may, upon request of the obligee or Public Office, order the obligor to name the child covered by the order as a beneficiary of any health insurance plan that is available to the obligor on a group basis, or as a beneficiary of an independent health insurance plan to be obtained by the obligor, after considering the following factors:

(A) the medical needs of the child;

(B) the availability of a plan to meet those needs; and

(C) the cost of such a plan to the obligor.

(2) If the employer or labor union or trade union offers more than one plan, the order shall require the obligor to name the child as a beneficiary of the plan in which the obligor is enrolled.

(3) Nothing in this Section shall be construed to limit the authority of the court to establish or modify a support order to provide for payment of expenses, including deductibles, copayments and any other health expenses, which are in addition to expenses covered by an insurance plan of which a child is ordered to be named a beneficiary pursuant to this Section.

(c) Implementation and enforcement. (1) When the court order requires that a minor child be named as a beneficiary of a health insurance plan, other than a health insurance plan available through an employer or labor union or trade union, the obligor shall provide written proof to the obligee or Public Office that the required insurance has been obtained, or that application for insurance has been made, within 30 days of receiving notice of the court order. Unless the obligor was present in court when the order was issued, notice of the order shall be given pursuant to Illinois Supreme Court Rules. If an obligor fails to provide the required proof, he may be held in contempt of court.

(2) When the court requires that a minor child be named as a beneficiary of a health insurance plan available through an employer or labor union or trade union, ,the court's order shall be implemented in accordance with Section 706.1, as now or hereafter amended.

(d) Failure to maintain insurance. The dollar amount of the premiums for court-ordered health insurance, or that portion of the premiums for which the obligor is responsible in the case of insurance provided under a group health insurance plan through an employer or labor union or trade union where the employer or labor union or trade union pays a portion of the premiums, shall be considered an additional child support obligation owed by the obligor. When the obligor fails to provide or maintain health insurance pursuant to an order for support, the obligor shall be liable to the obligee for the dollar amount of the premiums which were not paid, and shall also be liable for all medical expenses incurred by the minor child which would have been paid or reimbursed by the health insurance which the obligor was ordered to provide or maintain. In addition, the obligee may petition the court to modify the order based solely on the obligor's failure to pay the premiums for court-ordered health insurance.

(e) Authorization for payment. The signature of the obligee is a valid authorization to the insurer to process a claim for payment under the insurance plan to the provider of the health care services or to the obligee.

(f) Disclosure of information. The obligor's employer or labor union or trade union shall disclose to the obligee or Public Office, upon request, information concerning any dependent coverage plans which would be made available to a new employee or labor union member or trade union member. The employer or labor union or trade union shall disclose such information whether or not a court order for medical support has been entered.

PART VI—CUSTODY

5/602. Best interest of child

§ 602. Best Interest of Child. (a) The court shall determine custody in accordance with the best interest of the child. The court shall consider all relevant factors including:

(1) the wishes of the child's parent or parents as to his custody;

(2) the wishes of the child as to his custodian;

(3) the interaction and interrelationship of the child with his parent or parents, his siblings and any other person who may significantly affect the child's best interest;

(4) the child's adjustment to his home, school and community;

(5) the mental and physical health of all individuals involved;

(6) the physical violence or threat of physical violence by the child's potential custodian, whether directed against the child or directed against another person;

(7) the occurrence of ongoing abuse as defined in Section 103 of the Illinois Domestic Violence Act of 1986,[2] whether directed against the child or directed against another person; and

(8) the willingness and ability of each parent to facilitate and encourage a close and continuing relationship between the other parent and the child.

(b) The court shall not consider conduct of a present or proposed custodian that does not affect his relationship to the child.

(c) The court shall presume that the maximum involvement and cooperation of both parents regarding the physical, mental, moral, and emotional well-being of their child is in the best interest of the child. However, such presumption shall not be construed as a presumption that an order awarding joint custody is in the best interests of the child.

5/602.1. Parental powers—Joint custody—Criteria

§ 602.1 (a) The dissolution of marriage, the declaration of invalidity of marriage, the legal separation of the parents, or the parents living separate and apart shall not diminish parental powers, rights, and responsibilities except as the court for good reason may determine under the standards of Section 602.

(b) Upon the application of either or both parents, or upon its own motion, the court shall consider an award of joint custody. Joint custody means custody determined pursuant to a Joint Parenting Agreement or a Joint Parenting Order. In such cases, the court shall initially request the parents to produce a Joint Parenting Agreement. Such Agreement shall specify each parent's powers, rights and responsibilities for the personal care of the child and for major decisions such as education, health care, and religious training. The Agreement shall further specify a procedure by which proposed changes, disputes and alleged breaches may be mediated or otherwise resolved and shall provide for a periodic review of its terms by the parents. In producing a Joint Parenting Agreement, the parents shall be flexible in arriving at resolutions which further the policy of this State as expressed in Sections 102 and 602. For the purpose of assisting the court in making a determination whether an award of joint custody is appropriate, the court may order mediation and may direct that an investigation be conducted pursuant to the provisions of Section 605. In the event the parents fail to produce a Joint Parenting Agreement, the court may enter an appropriate Joint Parenting Order under the standards of Section 602 which shall specify and contain the same elements as a Joint Parenting Agreement, or it may award sole custody under the standards of Sections 602, 607, and 608.

(c) The court may enter an order of joint custody if it determines that joint custody would be in the best interests of the child, taking into account the following:

(1) the ability of the parents to cooperate effectively and consistently with each other towards the best interest of the child;

(2) the residential circumstances of each parent; and

(3) all other factors which may be relevant to the best interest of the child.

(d) Nothing within this section shall imply or presume that joint custody shall necessarily mean equal parenting time. The physical residence of the child in joint custodial situations shall be determined by:

(1) express agreement of the parties; or

(2) order of the court under the appropriate circumstances listed herein.

(e) Notwithstanding any other provision of law, access to records and information pertaining to a child, including but not limited to medical, dental, child care and school records, shall not be denied to a parent for the reason that such parent is not the child's custodial parent; however, no parent shall have access to the school records of a child if the parent is prohibited by an order of protection from inspecting or obtaining such records pursuant to the Illinois Domestic Violence Act of 1986, as now or hereafter amended.

1.   720 ILCS 5/12-4, 5/12-4.1, 5/12-4.2, 5/12-4.3, 5/12-13, 5/12-14, 5/12-15, or 5/12-16.

2.   750 ILCS 60/103.

CHILDREN AND DIVORCE BIBLIOGRAPHY

This list was compiled by and is reprinted with the permission of Virginia Simons, Licensed Clinical Social Worker, Evanston Family Therapy Center, and Chicago Center for Family Health Divorce Program.

BIBLIOGRAPHY FOR PROFESSIONALS

Adler, Robert. *Sharing the Children: How to Resolve Custody Problems and Get On with Your Life*. Bethesda, Md.: Adler & Adler, 1988.

Ahrons, Constance, and Rodgers, Roy. *Divorced Families: Meeting the Challenge of Divorce and Remarriage*. New York: Norton, 1987.

Barris, Mitchell, and Garrty, C. *Children of Divorce: A Developmental Approach to Residence and Visitation*. DeKalb, Ill.: Psytec, 1988.

Berne, P., and Savory, L. *Building Self-Esteem in Children*. New York: Continuum, 1987.

Dreikus, Rudolf. *Children: The Challenge*. New York: Dutton, 1964.

Furstenber, F., and Cherlin, Andrew. *Divided Families: What Happens to Children When Parents Part*. Cambridge, Mass.: Harvard Univ. Press, 1991.

Gesell, Arnold; Frances, Ilg; and Ames, Louise Bates. *The Child from Zero to Five / Five to Ten / Ten to Fifteen* (Gesell Inst. Series), Revised ed. New York: Harper & Row, 1977.

Isaacs, Marla; Montalvo, Braulio; and Ableson, David. *The Difficult Divorce: Therapy for Children and Families*. New York: Basic Books, 1986.

Johnston, Janet, and Campbell, Linda. *Impasses of Divorce: The Dynamics and Resolution of Family Conflict*. New York: Free Press, 1988.

Kalter, Neil. *Growing Up with Divorce*. New York: Free Press, 1990.

Kressel, Kenneth. *The Process of Divorce: How Professionals and Couples Negotiate Divorce*. New York: Basic Books, 1985.

Leach, P. *Your Baby & Child*. New York: Knopf, 1983.

Sager, Clifford; Brown, Hollis; Crohn, Helen; Engel, Tamara; Rodstein, Evelyn; and Walker, Libby. *Treating the Remarried Family*. New York: Brunner-Mazel, 1983.

Saposnek, Donald T. *Mediating Child Custody Disputes*. San Francisco: Jossey-Bass, 1985.

Visher, Emily, and Visher, John. *Old Loyalties, New Ties, Therapeutic Strategies with Stepfamilies*. New York: Brunner-Mazel, 1988.

Wallerstein, Judith, and Kelly, Joan. *Surviving the Breakup*. New York: Basic Books, 1980.

BIBLIOGRAPHY FOR CHILDREN AND PARENTS

Adler, Robert. *Sharing the Children: How to Resolve Custody Problems and Get On with Your Life*. Bethesda, Md.: Adler & Adler, 1988.

Alexander, A. *To Live a Lie*. New York: Atheneum, 1975. (6–11 yrs).

Barris, Mitchell, and Garrty, C. *Children of Divorce: A Developmental Approach to Residence and Visitation*. DeKalb, Ill.: Psytec, 1988.

Blume, J. *It's Not the End of the World*. New York: Bradbury, 1972. (10–13 yrs).

Berman, Claire. *What Am I Doing in a Step Family?* Secaucus, N. J.: Life Stewart, 1982. (6–11 yrs).

Berne, P., and Savory, L. *Building Self-Esteem in Children*. New York: Continuum, 1987.

Brown, L., and Brown, M. *The Dinosaur's Divorce*. New York: Trumpet Club, 1988. Paperback (Preschool to 8–9 yrs).

Dreikus, Rudolf. *Children: The Challenge*. New York: Dutton, 1964.

Gesell, Arnold; Frances, Ilg; and Ames, Louise Bates. *The Child from Zero to Five / Five to Ten / Ten to Fifteen* (Gesell Inst. Series), Revised ed. New York: Harper & Row, 1977.

Hyde, Margaret. *My Friend Has Four Parents*. New York: McGraw-Hill, 1981. (6–11 yrs).

Jewett, C. *Helping Children Cope with Separation and Loss*. Boston: Harvard Common Press, 1982.

Krementz, J. *How It Feels When Parents Divorce*. New York: Knopf, 1984. (6–11 yrs).

Leach, P. *Your Baby & Child*. New York: Knopf, 1983.

Magle, P. *Why Are We Getting a Divorce?* New York: Harmony Books, 1988. (3–7 yrs).

Ricci, Isolina. *Mom's House, Dad's House: Making Shared Custody Work.* New York: Macmillan, 1980. (Ricci's book is a classic. Her emphasis is on *shared* parenting rather than the formal designation of custody.)

Richards, A., and Willis, I. *How to Get It Together When Your Parents Are Coming Apart.* New York: McKay, 1976. (Adolescents).

Rofes, E. *The Kid's Book of Divorce: By, For, and About Kids.* New York: Vintage Books, 1982. (Early to mid-adolescents and their parents).

SUGGESTED READING LIST FOR DIVORCED PARENTS AND THEIR CHILDREN

This Bibliography was compiled by and is reprinted with the permission of the Children First Foundation, 307 East Washington Street, Belleville, Illinois 62220.

BIBLIOGRAPHY FOR PARENTS

Bonkowski, S. *Kids Are Nondivorceable.* Chicago: Buckley Publications, 1987.

A workbook for divorced parents and their children.

Ciborowski, Paul J. *The Changing Family I.* New York: Stratmar Educational Systems, 1984.

A resource manual which includes over 30 small-group and classroom activities for children (ages 11–17) from divorced homes.

Diamond, Sandra A. *Helping Children of Divorce: A Handbook for Parents and Teachers.* New York: Schocken, 1985.

Excellent guide for working effectively with schools.

Dodson, Fitzhugh. *How to Single Parent.* New York: Harper & Row, 1987.

Fisher, Bruce. *Rebuilding: When Your Relationship Ends.* San Luis Obispo, Calif.: Impact Publishers, 1981.

Textbook often used for divorce adjustment seminars.

Faber, A., and Mazlish, E. *How to Talk So Kids Will Listen and Listen So Kids Will Talk.* New York: Avon, 1982.

Franke, Linda Bird. *Growing Up Divorced.* New York: Simon & Schuster, 1983.

Describes the various stages children and teens go through in reaction to parental divorce; an excellent book for parents.

Friedman, James. *The Divorce Handbook: Your Guide to Divorce.* New York: Random House, 1981.

Excellent resource for understanding how the legal system functions.

Gardner, Richard A. *The Parents Book about Divorce.* New York: Doubleday, 1977.

Written in a popular vein, it gives parents an idea of the dynamics at work in their children during and after divorce.

Grollman, Earl, ed. *Explaining Divorce to Children.* Boston: Beacon Press, 1969.

Contributors to the book cover topics such as practical rules for telling children about divorce; religious views of divorce; parental dating.

Krantzler, Mel. *Creative Divorce: A New Opportunity for Personal Growth.* New York: M. Evans, 1974.

A classic for understanding the stages in the parent's emotional adjustment process.

Krementz, Jill. *How It Feels When Parents Divorce.* New York: Knopf, 1984.

Gives examples of children from various age groups and what they have to say about the divorce experience; a view from the child's perspective.

Lansky, Vicki. *Vicki Lansky's Divorce Book for Parents.* New York: New America Library, 1989.

A book every divorcing parent should have.

Ricci, Isolina. *Mom's House, Dad's House: Making Shared Custody Work.* New York: Macmillan, 1980.

A soon-to-be-revised guidebook for understanding how joint custody can work.

Salk, L. *What Every Child Would Like Parents to Know about Divorce.* New York: Harper & Row, 1978.

Spilke, Francine. *What About the Children?* New York: Crown, 1979.

A manual for parents that answers many questions raised by a divorce, such as telling your child about the divorce, dating, and remarriage.

Teyber, Edward. *Helping Your Children with Divorce.* New York: Pocket Books, 1985.

Turrow, Rita. *Daddy Doesn't Live Here Anymore.* Matteson, Ill: Great Lakes Living Press, 1977.

Discusses the emotional effects of divorce on children and suggests ways of helping them adjust to a family in transition.

Virtue, Doreen. *My Kids Don't Live with Me Any More.* Minneapolis: CompCare, 1988.

Visher, E., and Visher, J. *How to Win as a Stepfamily.* New York: Dembner, 1982.

Wallerstein, J., and Blakeslee, S. *Second Chances. Men, Women, and Children a Decade after Divorce.* New York: Ticknor & Fields, 1989.

Woolever, E., ed. *Your Child: Living with Divorce.* Better Homes & Gardens Book. Des Moines, Iowa: Meredith Books, 1990.

Divorce is never easy, even if everyone involved has decided it's for the best. This book gives you helpful information to guide you through the process from the initial stages to preparing to remarry and build a stepfamily.

BOOKS FOR PRESCHOOL AND EARLY ELEMENTARY CHILDREN

Adams, F. *Mushy Eggs.* New York: Putnam, 1973.

The story of a family managing well after divorce; fiction for children; preschool/beginning readers.

Boegehold, Betty. *Daddy Doesn't Live Here Anymore.* Racine, Wis.: Western Publishing, 1985.

Casey, a young girl whose parents divorce, is forced to accept the reality of her dad's leaving home; has many pictures.

Brown, L., and Brown, M. *Dinosaurs Divorce: A Guide for Changing Families*. Boston: Little, Brown, 1986.

Hazen, B. S. *Two Homes to Live In: A Child's-Eye View of Divorce*. New York: Human Sciences Press, 1978.

This is a picture book; through the eyes of Niki, we see a child struggle with the issues of loyalty, abandonment, and anger; a child's view of divorce.

Ives, S.; Fassler D.; and Lash, M. *The Divorce Workbook*. Burlington, Vt.: Waterfront Books, 1985.

For parents and children to use together; it explains separation, divorce, and remarriage; space is provided for drawing and coloring.

Lexau, Joan. *Emily and the Klunky Baby and the Next Door Dog*. New York: Dial, 1972.

Emily feels neglected by her mom and tries to find her dad. Her feelings and anxieties are finally resolved in a positive way; has good messages for kids.

Magid, K., and Schreibman, W. *Divorce Is... A Kid's Coloring Book*. Gretna, La.: Pelican, 1980.

25 common divorce-related issues are presented and paired with alternate resolutions; there are big drawings for children to color.

Mayle, Peter. *Divorce Can Happen to the Nicest People*. New York: Macmillan, 1980.

This is an illustrated handbook that deals with emotional issues, such as the hurt of divorce, starting a new life with one parent, and how to help oneself grow.

Sinbert, Janet. *Divorce Is a Grown-up Problem*. New York: Avon, 1978.

This is a lap book for parent and child; it uses illustrations to explain separation and divorce.

Stenson, Janet Sinbert. *Now I Have a Step-parent and It's Kind of Confusing*. New York: Avon, 1979.

A picture book for young children in a blended family.

Stinson, Kathy. *Mom and Dad Don't Live Together Any More*. Toronto: Annick Press, 1984.

Soft watercolors illustrate this little girl's description of her family's transition to joint custody parenting.

Watson, J.; Switzer, R.; and Hirshberg, J. *Sometimes a Family Has to Split Up*. New York: Crown, 1988.

Zindel, Paul. *I Love My Mother*. New York: Harper & Row, 1975.

A small boy talks about his single-parent mother; his mom not only cooks but teaches him to kick a football.

BOOKS FOR ADVANCED AND UPPER ELEMENTARY CHILDREN

Auch, Mary Jane. *Mom Is Dating Weird Wayne*. New York: Holiday House, 1988.

Blue, Rose. *A Month of Sundays*. New York: Franklin Watts, 1972.

A 10-year-old boy struggles to accept a move to New York with his mom after a parental divorce.

Blume, Judy. *It's Not the End of the World*. New York: Bradbury, 1972.

Karen and her sister cope with their feelings after their parent's divorce; her goal is to bring them back together again.

Brogan, J., and Maiden, U. *The Kids' Guide to Divorce*. New York: Fawcett, 1986.

An easy, conversational book that discusses the practical issues that effect children.

Cleary, Beverly. *Dear Mr. Henshaw*. New York: Morrow, 1983.

Clymer, Eleanor. *Lucie Was There*. New York: Rinehart & Winston, 1973.

Chronicles a young boy's search for security after his father and stepfather leave home; story takes place in a city and urban backdrop.

Danziger, Paula. *Divorce Express*. New York: Delacorte, 1982.

Ewing, Kathryn. *A Private Matter*. New York: Harcourt Brace Jovanovich, 1975.

Marcy, a 10-year-old girl, "adopts" an elderly man next door for affection and companionship; finally she accepts her parent's divorce and mom's remarriage.

Fassler, D.; Lash, M.; and Ives, S. B. *Changing Families: A Guide for Kids/Grown-ups*. Burlington, Vt.: Waterfront Books, 1988.

For use by children ages 4–12 with the support of caring adults, the interactive workbook helps children share their feelings and guides them through separation, divorce, child custody, support, visitation, remarriage, and new families.

Gardner, Richard. *The Boys' and Girls' Book about Divorce*. New York: Bantam, 1970.

Hunter, Evan. *Me and Mr. Stenner*. New York: Lippincott, 1976.

This is the story of an 11-year-old girl coping with her mother's divorce and remarriage. She learns to accept the new man whom her mother will marry, and finds that she can love her stepfather and real father at the same time.

Ives, S. B.; Fassler, D.; and Lash, M. *The Divorce Workbook: A Guide for the Kids and Families*. Burlington, Vt.: Waterfront Books, 1985.

Jong, Erica. *Megan's Book of Divorce*. New York: New American Library, 1984.

Precocious 4-year-old Megan tells her side of the story of her parents' separation and her enlightened joint custody situation.

LeShan, E. *What Makes Me Feel This Way?* New York: Macmillan, 1972.

In this book, emotions are identified and discussed in terms that children can understand; a book for parents and children to read together.

LeShan, E. *What's Going to Happen to Me?* New York: Four Winds, 1979.

This book offers children a positive approach to divorce and may help children to discuss feelings about divorce with parents.

Mann, P. *My Dad Lives in a Downtown Hotel*. New York: Doubleday, 1973.

Since both parents are careful to assure him they do not blame one another for their divorce, Joey concludes that HE is the cause. Gradually Joey learns to face reality and cope with life as it is.

Mayle, Peter. *Why Are We Getting a Divorce?* New York: Crown, 1978/88.

With a blend of humor, sensitivity, and fun illustrations, this book covers many difficult issues with objectivity.

Newfield, Marcia. *A Book for Jodan.* New York: Atheneum, 1975.

Jodan, age nine, doesn't believe her parents' reassurances of their love for her after their separation. Both parents work to promote her constructive adjustment, even though her father lives across the county. The book details an excellent, creative project for fathers.

Okomoto, Jean D. *My Mother Is Not Married to My Father.* New York: Pocket Books, 1979.

Park, B. *Don't Make Me Smile.* New York: Knopf, 1981.

Charles, 10 years old, refuses to attend school and runs away after a parental divorce; parents are insensitive to his anger.

Rofes, Eric. *The Kids' Book of Divorce: By, For, and About Kids.* Lexington, Mass.: Lewis Publishing, 1981.

Sanford, Doris. *Please Come Home.* Portland, Oreg.: Multnomeh, 1985.

Lovely color illustrations about an 8-year-old girl who wonders what will happen to her now that her daddy has gone.

Seuling, Barbara. *What Kind of Family Is This?* Racine, Wis.: Western Publishing, 1985.

Jeff, a young boy, moves into a new house when his mom remarries; discusses his ability to adjust to a stepdad and stepsiblings.

Simon, Norma. *I Wish I Had My Father.* Niles, Ill.: Albert Whitman, 1983.

For children who struggle with the feelings of rejection and sadness caused by a parent who has left them.

Sitea, L. *Zachary's Divorce* In *Free to Be Me.* New York: McGraw-Hill, 1974.

This entire book is an absolutely delightful look at children's emotions and values aimed at self-acceptance. Zachary's story about "his" divorce is simple, but captures the feelings of a small boy.

Snyder, Zilpha K. *Headless Cupid*. New York: Atheneum, 1971.

David, 11 years old, and his little brothers and sisters, have to adjust to the children of dad's new wife.

Williams, Barbara. *Mitzi's Honeymoon with Nana Potts*. New York: Dutton, 1983.

BOOKS FOR TEENS

Alexander, Ann. *To Live a Lie*. New York: Atheneum, 1975.

A 12-year-old girl imagines herself unloved and unwanted by divorcing parents; she lies and fibs to give herself a new identify and name.

Berger, Terry. *How Does It Feel When Your Parents Get Divorced?* New York: Messner, 1976.

A young girl deals with anger, fear, and sadness; includes pictures to help express these feelings that resulted from parental separation.

Booher, Dianna D. *Coping When Your Family Falls Apart*. New York: Messner, 1979.

A "can do" book that offers plenty of suggestions to meet practical problems that face teens after the breakup.

Burt, M., and Burt, R. *What's Special about Our Stepfamily*. New York: Dolphin Books, 1983.

A unique look at a stepfamily living together makes this book a must for those youngsters soon to be, or new in, a blended family.

Cameron, Eleanor. *To the Green Mountain*. New York: Dutton, 1975.

Kathy lives with her mother, who makes the painful decision to divorce her dad.

Corcoran, B. *Hey, That's My Soul You're Stomping On*. New York: Atheneum, 1978.

Rachel, 10 years old, lives with her grandparents during a parental divorce; focuses on her mixed feelings in returning to live with her mom.

Danzier, Paula. *The Divorce Express*. New York: Delacorte, 1982.

In this humorous novel about a joint custody family, Phoebe spends weekdays with her father in the suburbs and commutes back to the city to be with her mother for weekends on a bus called the "divorce express."

Fox, Paula. *The Moonlight Man*. New York: Dell, 1988.

Getzoff, A., and McClenahan, C. *Teenagers in Stepfamilies*. New York: Walker & Co., 1984.

Girion, Barbara. *Tangle of Roots*. New York: Putnam, 1985.

Klein, Norma. *Taking Sides*. New York: Pantheon, 1974.

Nell, 12 years old, adjusts to life with her father and 5-year-old brother after her parent's divorce; father is portrayed as a nurturing person.

Klein, Norma. *Mom, the Wolfman and Me*. New York: Pantheon, 1972.

Brett and her mom, who has never married, live a happy but nontraditional life. She worries about the changes that may occur if her mom marries.

Krementz, Jill. *How It Feels When Parents Divorce*. New York: Knopf, 1984.

In this moving book, beautifully illustrated with the author's photographs, twenty girls and boys from ages 7 to 16 express their feelings about their parents' divorce.

LeShan, Eda. *What's Going to Happen to Me?* New York: Four Winds, 1978.

In simple language, many questions about divorce are answered. Which parent will you live with? Will your parents remarry? Will they still be friends?

List, Julie. *The Day the Loving Stopped: A Daughter's View of Her Parents' Divorce*. New York: Seaview Books, 1980.

Julie tells about how she felt losing a day-to-day father and the disruption of living two lives—one with dad and one with mom.

Mann, Peggy. *My Dad Lives in a Downtown Hotel*. New York: Scholastic, 1973.

A young boy has strong feelings that he is responsible for his parent's divorce. How he deals with these feelings is the focus of this book.

Richards, A., and Willis, I. *How to Get It Together When Your Parents Are Coming Apart.* New York: Bantam, 1976.

A "coping" book that addresses those needing help with the stresses and confusion of parental divorce; includes an excellent section on legal aspects of divorce.

Rofes, Eric. *The Kid's Book of Divorce.* Lexington, Mass.: Lewis Publishing, 1981.

Children and young teens (ages 11–14) share their feelings and experiences on how their parents' separation/divorce affected them.

Sallis, Susan. *An Open Mind.* New York: Harper & Row, 1978.

Smith, Doris. *Kick a Stone Home.* New York: Crowell, 1974.

Sara Jane, 15 years old, still hopes her dad will come home after a divorce. She hates visiting him and his new wife and harbors resentment about his remarriage.

Sobol, Harriet L. *My Other—Mother, My Other—Father.* New York: Macmillan, 1979.

Andrea tells how she feels about being a stepchild and the difficulties and advantages of having two sets of parents; illustrations.

Stolz, Mary. *Leap before You Look.* New York: Harper & Row, 1972.

Tyler, Anne. *Dinner at the Homesick Restaurant.* New York: Knopf, 1982.

A story about two brothers and a sister who are deserted by their dad and raised by their angry mom; it moves through the stresses and joys of a difficult youth.

RESOURCES FOR MORE INFORMATION OR ASSISTANCE

These telephone numbers and addresses are for regional or statewide offices. The regional or statewide offices should be able to direct you to a local office that serves your area.

Illinois Lawyer Referral Service

A service of the Illinois State Bar Association. (800) 252-8916

This service can refer you to a lawyer in your area who will charge $15.00 for an initial half-hour consultation.

Legal Services Offices

Cook County Legal Assistance Foundation, Inc.

Serves Suburban Cook County (outside of Chicago).

Central Office - West
1146 Westgate, Suite 200
Oak Park, Illinois 60301
TDD (708) 524-2633
FAX (708) 524-2643
(708) 524-2600

Land of Lincoln Legal Assistance Foundation, Inc.

Serves the southern-most 65 counties in Illinois.

Executive Director's Office
2420 Bloomer Drive
Alton, Illinois 62002
FAX (618) 462-0043
(618) 462-0036

Legal Assistance Foundation of Chicago

General Office
343 South Dearborn, Room 700/800
Chicago, Illinois 60604
TDD (312) 341-1206
FAX (312) 341-1041
(312) 341-1070

Prairie State Legal Services, Inc.

Serves most of Northern and North Central Illinois outside of Cook County.

Administrative Office
975 North Main Street
Rockford, Illinois 61103-7064
TDD (815) 965-5114
FAX (815) 965-1081
(815) 965-2134

West Central Illinois Legal Assistance

Administrative Office
1614 East Knox Street
P.O. Box 1232
Galesburg, Illinois 61402-1232
Toll Free No. (800) 331-0617 (for clients only)
FAX (309) 343-7647
(309) 343-2141

Child Support Action Line

A service of the Division of Child Support Enforcement of the Illinois Department of Public Aid. Services are provided whether or not the custodial parent is a recipient of Public Aid. (800) 447-2278

Mental Health Agencies

For information on Mental Health Agencies in your area, call the Illinois Department of Mental Health and Developmental Disabilities at (800) 843-6154.

Social Service Agencies

Catholic Social Services

Provides services to people of all faiths. Local offices listed in phone directory under Catholic Social Services or Catholic Charities.

Illinois Department of Children and Family Services

For information on services provided by DCFS, contact the local office listed in your phone directory, or contact the state office at (217) 782-4000. To report abuse or neglect of a child, call (800) 252-2873.

Lutheran Social Services of Illinois

State headquarters provides services to people of all faiths.

1001 East Touhy Avenue, Suite 50
DesPlaines, Illinois 60018
(708) 635-4600

Domestic Violence Resource

Illinois Coalition Against Domestic Violence

This statewide office will be able to direct you to a shelter or advocate in your area.

937 South Fourth Street
Springfield, Illinois 62703
(217) 789-2830

NOTES

GLOSSARY

Abuse - Defined by the Illinois Domestic Violence Act as use of physical force and harassment, which is unreasonable conduct that would cause a reasonable person emotional distress.

Alternative dispute resolution - Reference to a number of methods of resolving disputes outside of a court contest. The methods include mediation and arbitration.

Antenuptial agreement - An agreement made by people before they were married with regard to how property be divided should those people divorce.

Annulment - A court order declaring that a marriage was void from the beginning and did not exist.

Arbitration - Use of a neutral third person outside the court process to resolve a dispute. Although the arbitrator is not a judge, the arbitrator does make a ruling like a judge would, which should resolve the issue.

Automatic stay - A new Illinois law which provides that neither party should make unnecessary expenditures nor should abuse or harass the other party after the divorce has been filed and the summons has been served.

Community property - A theory that some states use to divide property evenly upon divorce. Illinois is not a state that uses the community property theory.

Conciliation - An attempt to repair a broken marriage. A court can order two parties to attempt to get together by ordering a conciliation conference.

Default - When one party fails to respond within the time limit to a summons in a case.

Deposition - Questions to be answered in person under oath. A deposition is almost like a trial, but it is used in preparation for a trial.

Discovery - Processes by which your attorney can obtain information about your case, either from the other party, or from other witnesses who may have information.

Dissipation - When one spouse spends money on unnecessary items after the marriage has suffered a breakdown.

Dissolution - Divorce.

Emergency order of protection - An order prohibiting abuse and harassment that can last up to 21 days, and can be obtained without advance notice to the other party.

Ex parte - A hearing or conversation with a judge in which the other party to the dispute is not present.

First-stage hearing - The part of the divorce in which a judge hears evidence about grounds for the divorce.

Grounds - A reason to obtain a divorce.

Guardian ad litem - An attorney representing the best interests of the child to the court.

Harassment - Defined by the Illinois Domestic Violence Act as unnecessary conduct which would cause a reasonable person emotional distress.

In camera - An interview. A child may be asked questions in the judge's office.

Interim order of protection - An order prohibiting abuse and harassment which can last up to 30 days and can be granted only after the opposing party has received some notice of the court action.

Interrogatories - Written questions to be answered under oath by a party in the case.

Joint custody - An arrangement where parents share legal decision-making with regard to the children, and share physical care of the children in any number of ways.

Jurisdiction - Power of the court to act in regard to a particular person or piece of property.

Legal separation - A court order that is almost the same as a divorce, except that the parties remain legally married.

Maintenance - What used to be called alimony. Payment from one spouse to the other spouse after the marriage has ended.

Marital property - Property acquired during the marriage, except property acquired by gift or inheritance. See Chapter 8 for a more detailed discussion of marital and nonmarital property.

Mediation - Use of a neutral third person to help the two parties in a divorce reach an agreement of their own.

Mental cruelty - One of several grounds for obtaining a divorce.

Modification - Changing a court order.

No-fault divorce - This is often the phrase used to refer to a divorce based on irreconcilable differences. The parties must have been separated for at least six months to obtain a divorce this way.

Nonmarital property - Property that was acquired before the marriage, or that was acquired during the marriage by gift or inheritance. See Chapter 8 for a more detailed discussion of nonmarital and marital property.

Order for withholding - A court order which requires an employer to set aside a certain amount of money in each pay period for child support.

Plenary order of protection - An order prohibiting abuse or harassment that can last up to two years, or can be permanent if it is included in a divorce order.

Pro se - Latin for "for yourself." A person who is in court without an attorney is referred to as pro se.

Property - Can refer to either real estate or personal items, such as a car and furnishings.

Qualified domestics relations order - Also known as QDRO. An order that can reassign pension benefits from one spouse to another.

Removal - When a custodial parent wants to move with the children outside of the state of Illinois.

Rehabilitative maintenance - Also referred to as "temporary" maintenance. Payments made by one spouse to the other for a limited period of time in order to help that spouse to become self-sufficient.

Second-stage hearing - A hearing held after the judge has already found grounds for the divorce. All other issues remaining in the divorce should be considered in the second stage hearing.

Service - The delivery of a summons or other document. When the service is of a summons, it is frequently referred to as service of process.

Sole custody - An arrangement where one parent has the child or children for most of the time, and makes the important decisions regarding the child or children's lives.

Summons - A document given to a person against whom a case has been filed. The summons tells the person the name and number of the case, and how much time that person will have to file a response to the request for legal action.

Tender years presumption - A concept that was used in custody decisions many years ago that awarded custody of small children automatically to the mother unless the mother was unfit. This presumption does not apply now.

Transmutation - When nonmarital property is changed into marital property, for example, when two savings accounts held separately before marriage are combined into one joint savings account.

Uncontested - A divorce in which there is no disagreement as to the results that should be obtained.

NOTES

INDEX